HOW TO WRITE A BOOK

12 simple steps to becoming an author

Geoff Palmer

PODSNAP PUBLISHING
WELLINGTON NEW, ZEALAND

Podsnap Publishing Ltd., 17 Moir Street, Mt Victoria, Wellington 6011, New Zealand.

Published by Podsnap Publishing Ltd., 2019

Copyright © Geoff Palmer 2019

The author's moral right has been asserted.

Apart from fair dealing for the purposes of study, research, criticism or review, no part of this book may be reproduced or transmitted by any person or entity, in any form or by any means, electronic or mechanical, including photocopying, recording, scanning or by any information storage and retrieval system, without prior permission in writing from the publisher.

All rights reserved.

Cover photo: © Can Stock Photo / jstan

Acknowledgements

My grateful thanks to my beta readers
Sarah Cleland,
Chris Edwardes,
Nicola Price
and especially
Evan Thomas
for their invaluable comments, critiques
and encouragement.

Table of Contents

The thing about writing is not to talk, but to do it; no matter how bad or even mediocre it is, the process is the thing, not the sitting and theorizing about how one should write ideally, or how well one could write if one really wanted to or had the time.

— *Sylvia Plath,* Letters Home

Introduction..1
    An overview, or avoiding insanity..2

PART I: GETTING STARTED

1: Finding the Time to Write 7
    The ticking clock...7
    Tracking down lost time...9
        Results from Sally 11
        Results from Bob 11
        ... and your results?..12
    Making time..14
        The fallacy of goal setting..14
        Intention statements..17
    Writing with a tomato..18
        Here's how to "pomodoro"..19
    Carving out some *you* time...20

2: Avoiding Distractions 22
    The Problem: You may be looking at it................................22

The elephant in the room..24
The myth of multitasking...25
Software solutions..26
Hardware solutions...27
The sneakiest distraction of all...28
    A footnote..29
    A footnote to the footnote...30
The baby elephant in the room..30
Stopping the distraction attraction..30

3: Dealing with the Empty Page 33
Plotters vs pantsers...34
    A practical example..34
The seven basic plots..36
Characters and situations...38
Weaving a story...39

4: How Much Research Do I Need? 42
Listen to Lee Child..42
Fiction vs non-fiction..43
Makers of other worlds..44
How much background do you really need?..............................45
Putting worlds together...46

5: Doubt: Every Writer's Enemy 48
Writing classes (and other forms of lobotomy).........................51
Writing workshops..53
Class checklist..54

6: Getting in the Zone..57
Resistance...58
Turning pro..59
Production targets..60
    Don't break the chain..60

7: Writing's Dirty Little Secret 64
Ssshh, don't tell anyone this!...66
How *do* you get started?...67
Another writing secret...67
Don't start with number one...68
One-draft writers and Heinlein's Third Rule............................70

PART II : KEEPING GOING

8: Running Out of Steam 77
The myth of slow writing..79

9: How to Handle Writer's Block 83
Some common suggestions...85
    Freewriting...85
    Journaling...85
    Step away from the desk..85
    Don't go there in the first place..86

10: Changer Dangers 88
Lookout, Chekov's got a gun!...88
Rewriting (and rewriting, and rewriting)..................................89
A writing secret: Gun safety...91

PART III: LETTING GO

11: The Pursuit of Perfection 95
It has to be perfect...96
A general anxiety about whether the story works....................96
Worry about how people will judge you.................................96
It really is excrement...97
The practise novel...97
Get thee to an assessor!...98

12: Critical Overload 101
Handling rejection...101

You're not alone!..104
Another sort of lottery..106

BONUS CONTENT

Bonus Chapter..**109**
    Write what you love..109
    Treat it like a business...110
        A very important footnote..112
    Become a guinea pig...112
    Do a Nanowrimo..114
        Footnote..116
    Wearing two hats...116
    practise, Productivity and Professionalism........................118
        practise...118
        Productivity...118
        Professionalism...119
    Being a successful writer..119

Appendix 1..**122**
    A handy word-count table...122

    About the Author...125
    About the Reader..126
    Also by Geoff Palmer..127

INDEX..129

Introduction

*"An incurable itch for scribbling takes possession of many,
and grows inveterate in their insane breasts."*
— *Juvenal (circa 100 AD)*

On 1 September 1995, Jim Grant sat down to write. He'd never written a novel before and, having just been made redundant from his job at Granada Television, reckoned he'd have to earn himself a laptop. So he went out and bought three pads of paper, a pencil, a pencil-sharpener and an eraser, investing the princely sum of £3.99 in his new vocation. Then settled down to work. Long-hand.

The book he wrote – called *Killing Floor* – earned Grant a laptop all right, and a great deal more. It, and his subsequent books, have regularly topped the bestseller charts for the last twenty years. But you probably don't recognise his name. That's because Grant writes under the pseudonym Lee Child.[1]

My aim in opening with that story wasn't to add to the mythology of Jim Grant/Lee Child, or to help him sell more books. (He seems to be doing okay without my assistance.) What I wanted to emphasise was the writer's basic tools:

- pads of paper
- a pencil

- a pencil-sharpener
- an eraser

That, really, is all you need. And it's all writers have needed for centuries.

It's easy to find reasons for *not* writing. You don't need a new laptop with terabytes of disk space and monitor large enough to be seen from the Moon. All you really need is £3.99's worth of supplies. (About $5 in the US.)

If you have a typewriter, great. A computer of some sort's even better. But neither of those things are essential. All you need is some method of recording your thoughts. A pencil and paper work fine. Just ask Lee Child.

> ## Fiction or non-fiction
>
> These days, I mainly write fiction, and that's the general slant of this book, but most of the tips and techniques discussed here apply to all types of writing, whether it's a thesis, a short story, a family history or a novel.

An overview, or avoiding insanity

"A non-writing writer is a monster courting insanity."
— *Franz Kafka*

The aim of this book is to help you avoid insanity by addressing the common myths that surround writing and the writing process. In particular, it addresses our capacity for self-deception: the little lies we tell ourselves; the tricks the mind can play on us. (Like, "I really need a new computer first ...")

Writing can be hard work, but not in the sense of digging a ditch or mixing cement. As I write this, Council rubbish collectors are doing the weekly street collection outside my front window. It's winter. An icy southerly is lashing at them with whip-cracks of horizontal rain. You can sense the weariness in their movements, see it in their faces. They've been battling the storm all day. Meanwhile, I sit watching from my cosy office, nursing a cup of tea and contemplating this introduction. "You think you've got it tough?" I tell them. Quietly.

This book is divided into three sections. Part I: Getting Started is where most beginners have most problems; finding the time, dealing with uncertainty, getting underway and so on. But starting doesn't mean you'll finish. In fact, the vast majority of books started are abandoned at around the one-third mark. We'll look at why in Part II: Keeping Going.

The tricks of the mind don't stop there either. Even after you've typed THE END you'll find more reasons why your book is still not quite finished. We'll deal with those in Part III: Letting Go.

Now, let's start dealing with your insanity ...

Footnotes:
[1] This story is recounted in *Reacher Said Nothing : Lee Child and the Making of Make Me*, by Andy Martin, **http://geoffpalmer.co.nz/htwab01**.

Part I

Getting Started

"Writing is not necessarily something to be ashamed of, but do it in private and wash your hands afterwards."

— *Robert Heinlein*

1: "I can't do that today!"

Finding the Time to Write

"Time unbound is hard to handle."
— May Sarton

We all lead busy lives and there are lots we'd like to do, but often can't fit it all in. Writing can be like that. A nice-to-do, even a want-to-do, yet somehow it becomes a never-quite-get-round-to-it.

Well, brace yourself. I'm about to let you into a nasty little secret; a time-swallowing monster that most of us aren't even aware of. Conquer it, even in a modest way, and in six months or a year's time, *you* could be thumbing through the first draft of a completed book.

There's no magic here. No mysteries. No arcane secrets. Nothing to buy. No special software or clever tools. All that's required is a little commonsense, a little thought, and a willingness to give it a go.

Are you with me?

The ticking clock

How long is a lifetime? Assuming you make it to 80 years of age, you'll clock up a little over 700,000 hours, or 4,100 weeks. What's more, you'll spend more than 1,300 of those weeks asleep.

Let's break it down further.

There are 168 hours in a week – seven days times 24 hours. Subtract a third (56 hours) for beddy-byes and we're left with just 112 hours in which to cram everything else.

1 week (7 days X 24 hours)	=	168 hours
minus		
Sleep time (7 days x 8 hours)	=	56 hours
Time Remaining	=	**112 hours**

A little over a hundred years ago, you'd have spent 70 of those 112 waking hours at work. Today, in most developed countries, the average work week is 30-40 hours, which leaves 72-82 hours unaccounted for.

Of course, we don't just sleep and work, so let's break it down some more:

Waking week	=	112 hours
minus		
Full-time work (5 days x 8 hours)	=	40 hours
Commuting (5 days x 1 hour each way)	=	10 hours
Time Remaining	=	**62 hours**

Let's also factor in meal breaks:

Carried forward	=	62 hours
minus		
Breakfast (7 days x 1 hour)	=	7 hours
Lunch (7 days x 1 hour)	=	7 hours
Dinner (7 days x 1 hour)	=	7 hours
Time Remaining	=	**41 hours**

What, you only spend ten minutes on breakfast and eat lunch on the run? Maybe you spend two hours preparing dinner and dining with a loved one. Bear with me. These figures are only rough. I'm making generalisations and being a little over-generous.

There's one thing missing from the above calculations and that's general living tasks like shopping, household chores, chilling out, meeting friends, playing with the kids, walking the dog, and ... well, having a life. Let's allow three hours a day for that ...

```
Carried forward                              =     41 hours
  minus
General living (7 days x 3 hours)            =     21 hours
Time Remaining                               =     20 hours
```

You probably don't spend six hours a week shopping, five hours chatting to friends and so on – or if you do they're often combined with other activities like commuting or weekday lunch hours. Remember, this is just a general estimate. The important figure is that bottom line. Even with an allowance of 21 hours for just feeding your face, it still leaves 20 hours a week free!

Let me repeat that: *20 hours a week, free!*

So where the hell does it go ...?

Tracking down lost time

The calculations above are broad and very general. What we really need is some specific data about *you*, your habits, your situation and your responsibilities. It's time for a little exercise.

Starting now, keep a timesheet. Whether or not you do it for a full week is optional. If one working day is pretty much like another, just record two or three of them. Weekends are often more varied, but again, what we're looking for is the *general pattern*. If you have a regular work-week then head off for a weekend's skiing, and you don't do that every weekend, pick a more regular weekend to record. Likewise, if you happen to be reading this while on a Caribbean cruise or touring Tibet by yak – and you don't normally do that – leave it till you get home.

Don't include every single thing calculated to the second. Just work in 15-minute blocks. And general headings like these will do:

- Sleep
- Personal grooming (showers, getting ready for work, make-up, haircuts, etc.)
- Household chores (grocery shopping, laundry, etc.)
- Caring for others (kids, elderly relatives, grandkids, etc.)
- Work
- Education and courses (outside of work, obviously)
- Meals (including preparation time and washing up)
- Travel or commuting
- Leisure time:
- Sports, exercise, recreation
- Relaxing
- Socialising (in person)
- Socialising (online: Facebook, Twitter, Pinterest, etc.)
- Computer use (playing games, browsing, news, etc.)
- Reading
- TV (broadcast television, Netflix, Hulu, Amazon, etc. whether watched on TV, phone, computer or tablet)
- Other leisure activities

Some of this stuff falls into what I call *double-up territory*. What about having lunch with a friend or checking Facebook from your desk? Just record whatever the *principle* activity was. (In these cases, *Meals* and *Work*.)

To make adding up easier, use decimals:

- 15 minutes = 0.25
- 30 minutes = 0.50
- 45 minutes = 0.75

So two-and-a-half hours plus three-and-three-quarter hours would look like: 2.50 + 3.75. (Which equals 6.25, or six-and-a-quarter hours.)

The key thing is *be honest*. If you spent 19 hours blobbing out watching re-runs of a favourite TV series, don't put it down to *Education*. The only person you're fooling is yourself.

Now get to work. See you in a few days time!

Results from Sally ...

Below you'll find a sample from a 24-year-old friend called Sally. Her days vary considerably, so she spent a full week recording things day by day.

```
Sleep                                             62.50
Personal grooming                                  8.00
Household chores                                   9.00
Caring for others                                  1.00
Work                                              35.00
Education                                          0.00
Meals                                             10.50
Travel or commuting                               11.50
Leisure time:
    - Sports, exercise, recreation     2.50
    - Relaxing                         1.00
    - Socialising (in person)          5.75
    - Socialising (online)             3.25
    - Computer use                     2.00
    - Reading                          0.00
    - TV (including video on demand)  15.00
    - Other leisure activities         1.00
Leisure sub-total                                 30.50
                      Total hours                168.00
```

Results from Bob ...

Bob is a 42-year-old whose work days don't vary much, so he just recorded two of them, averaged them out and multiplied by five to make up a working week. He did, however, keep a full record of his "typical" weekend:

Sleep		58.00
Personal grooming		4.50
Household chores		5.50
Caring for others		3.00
Work		47.00
Education		0.00
Meals		7.00
Travel or commuting		6.75
Leisure time:		
- Sports, exercise, recreation	2.00	
- Relaxing	0.00	
- Socialising (in person)	5.50	
- Socialising (online)	1.00	
- Computer use	1.00	
- Reading	2.00	
- TV (including video on demand)	24.00	
- Other leisure activities	0.75	
Leisure sub-total		36.25
Total hours		168.00

... and your results?

Assuming this was a typical week for you – there was no unexpected rush at work, no family crisis or other emergency – you'll now have a pretty good picture of where you spend your time, and your leisure time in particular. Most people are surprised. Some are horrified.

Your results may differ wildly from Bob and Sally's – there's no "correct" answer – but I suspect you'll have one thing in common with both of them; a good slice of your leisure time is spent watching television. According to *Business Insider*[1], "the average human being spends about 4 hours a day, or 28 hours a week, watching television."

> ## TV's Sneaky Secret
>
> Did you know that a typical TV hour is really only 43 minutes long? The rest is advertising, "station identification", previews and promos for upcoming shows – which are, of course, also advertising. So if you spend 28 hours a week in front of the goggle box, you're spending almost 8 hours watching ads!

And that's it. That's the time-sapping secret of most peoples' lives: they watch TV. (This includes broadcast, satellite, cable, video on demand, etc.) In fact, they spend almost as much time in front of the television as they spend at work.

Things are changing. TV viewing hours are dropping, particularly amongst younger people. But they're being replaced with time online: social networking, chatting, playing games, and so on.

> ## The Addiction Connection
>
> Ever wondered why TV movies have no ads in the first 15-20 minutes, or why you can seem to keep scrolling down Facebook forever? Two reasons: to get you hooked, and keep you there.
>
> TV networks know that anyone watching the first 15-20 minutes of a movie is probably going to see it through, so they can steadily increase the ad frequency. Which they do. (Ever notice how many ads you get near the end of a movie? That's not a

> coincidence!)
>
> The internet's no different. The reason Facebook appears to be bottomless is that eternal scrolling-down suggests, "Hey, there's still more to see yet." Likewise, if you visit YouTube and watch a video clip, once it's over the site will automatically start another, related one. (Unless you click to cancel it.) The idea in both cases is to keep you there, improve the quality of the data they collect about you, and, hopefully, sell you more stuff.
>
> These aren't chance developments. Big websites and TV networks consult psychologists to improve their addiction profiles.

So what can we do about it? How can we fight all these things that are conspiring to suck up our precious leisure time?

That's what we're here for. Onward!

Making time

First, the bad news: If you want to write, no one is going to hand you a box of time in which to do so. You're going to have to find that time yourself. The good news is that it's not that difficult. Armed with the knowledge of where your time's currently going, we can start to make some headway.

What follows are a few simple techniques to get you started on the path of regular writing. But first, let's slay a common myth.

The fallacy of goal setting

Despite what everyone tells you, setting goals is mostly a waste of time, and in many cases it's self-defeating. Imagine, for example, you set yourself a goal of going to the gym five times a week. Exercise can be hard work, particularly when you're starting out, and especially if you already put a lot of energy into your job. Most people don't really enjoy gym workouts and only go along because they feel they have to. The least temptation – a couple of drinks after work, catching up with a friend, a cold, a late night the night before – and you'll skip a session, promising yourself you'll catch up at the weekend, or next week ... yet somehow you never do. Pretty soon, that daily workout's down to three times a week, then two, then none.

Sound familiar? Yep, we've all done it.

(It's also the reason why gyms sell memberships, not one-trip tickets. It guarantees their income because only 18% of members use the gym regularly and consistently.[2])

Many years ago I joined a company that had a corporate gym. I went along and did a fitness test, pedalling a stationary bicycle for a fixed number of minutes before having my pulse and respiratory rate checked to see how quickly I recovered. The fitness instructor graphed my results and said, 'So what sports do you play?'

'Sports? Me?' I laughed. 'I don't.'

'Something social, then: jogging, swimming, surfing, social football?'

I shook my head.

He looked puzzled and checked his graph again. 'Are you sure?'

'I ski a bit in the winter. A week, maybe. And the occasional weekend.'

He shook his head. 'It won't be that. You must be doing *something* regularly.'

I racked my brains. 'I do walk to work each day.'

'How far?'

'It's about twenty minutes each way.'

He threw up his hands. 'There you go. You're doing two workouts a day!'

Two workouts a day? I'd never guessed. And if someone had told me I *had* to do two workouts a day (or even one), my answer would have turned their ears blue.

What I'd lucked into by pure chance was a *system*, not a goal. That system carried me to and from work each day. I never once thought of walking as a workout – and I still don't. It's a way to get somewhere, certainly, but it's also a time to think, to meet people and chat, listen to music or an audiobook. It's not dependent on anything. There are no scheduled classes, no start and stop times. I can head out early and dawdle, work late, have a drink afterwards, go to a movie and dinner, and still complete my workout for the day. I don't think of it as a part of an exercise regime or a scheme for healthy living. It's just what I do.

It passes what I call the Toothbrush Test.

No one ever agonises over brushing their teeth. No one goes,"I'm not in the mood to brush right now," or "I'm too tired," or "I'll double-brush tomorrow." They just do it without agonising over it, or even really thinking about it. It's a habit. An ingrained system: *Going to bed? Brush teeth. Morning shower? Brush teeth.*

If you can sneak writing into your daily routine and make it a habit, you're on your way. For many years I set my alarm an hour earlier than I really needed for work and got into the habit of writing before breakfast. It became an unthinking part of my routine. I just did it.

Here's another reason why goals aren't helpful. Consider these worthy aims:

- In two years' time, I'm going to have my boss's job.
- I'm going to lose 20lb/10Kg's by Christmas.
- This year I'm going to write a novel.

What's missing here?

You probably spotted it right away. That's right, the *how*. *How* do you plan to get your boss's job in two years' time? *How* are you going to lose that much weight? *How* will you go about writing a novel?

Now consider these alternatives:

- I'm going to build my knowledge and qualifications by doing part-time courses in business administration, accountancy and IT.
- Instead of buying a two-zone bus ticket each month, I'm going to buy a one-zone ticket and walk that extra zone.
- Every work day, I'm going to write 300 words during my lunch break.

See the difference? Systems, not goals. Simple practices that will lead you to your goals – and maybe way beyond. Concrete things you can start doing right away.

Intention statements

A practical way to get a system like this going is to use Intention Statements, simple declarations of what, when and where you will undertake a task. Use this format:

During the next week, I will [ACTION]
on [DAY]
[TIME OF DAY]
at/in [PLACE].

For example, a would-be writer might declare:

During the next week, I will write at least 300 words
every working day
starting at 6:00 am
in my home office.

Or:

*During the next week, I will write for 30 minutes
on every work-day lunch break
starting at 12:15
in the library near my workplace.*

There are three key points to remember:

- **Be specific.** Research shows that 91% of people who write their intention statements out fully end up following through, compared with only 35% of people who don't plan the where and when.
- **Be reasonable.** Choose an action you think you can achieve and sustain. 300 words in an hour is reasonable (and notice that "at least"), whereas 3,000 words isn't.
- **Set a daily reminder.** Set a reminders on your phone or calendar every Sunday. This not only adds a gentle call to action, but it reminds you to plan for weeks when things don't go as planned. Perhaps you've got a heavy work commitment coming up or have to travel. It gives you a chance to modify your plan ahead of time – which enhances your sense of control.

Writing with a tomato

Now you've set aside a slice of time, you might consider the Pomodoro Technique, a method of time-management many writers find useful. It was developed by Francesco Crillo in the 1980's and takes its name from the tomato-shaped kitchen timer Crillo originally used. (Pomodoro is Italian for "tomato".)

There's a whole website[3] devoted to it, but you really only need three items to get started:

- A pencil.
- A piece of paper.

- A timer of some sort.

You can use a timing app on your computer or phone, but I prefer a mechanical kitchen timer – the type you twist and set[4]. There are a number of reasons for "going analogue". If you're working on a computer, you really don't want any more distractions on it, (see the next chapter), and your phone should be silenced and shut in a drawer for the same reason. There's something about the physical action of twisting and setting the timer that helps me focus on the task, and I find the quiet tick-tick-tick in the background a subtle prompt to keep going.

A *pomodoro* is 25-minutes long. *It is absolutely indivisible!* There's no such thing as a half-pomodoro or three-fifths of one. If you don't complete a pomodoro, it's just not counted.

Here's how to "pomodoro"

- Decide on a task; writing, revising, editing, etc.
- Set the timer for 25 minutes.
- Work on the task until the timer rings.
- When it rings, put a tick on the piece of paper.
- If you have fewer than four ticks, take a five-minute break then go back to Step 2.
- If you've accumulated four ticks, put a line through them to cancel them out and take a 15-20 minute break. When you return, go back to Step 1.

Think back to the quote at the beginning of this chapter: *Time unbound is hard to handle*. And it is! If the boss gives you a week to write a report, you can bet it'll take a week, but if he wants it by tomorrow ...

The advantage of working this way is that it breaks time into manageable units which helps you keep focused. ("No, I won't check my email till the timer rings.") What's more, the pomodoros don't have to be contiguous. I know of one writer who makes her four-a-day by doing two in the morning before work, one at lunchtime, and one in the evening. Writer Kat Loterzo credits the technique with helping her draft a book in just three weeks.[5]

What you do in the breaks is up to you. Check your phone, meditate, do a little light exercise, grab some fresh air ... My preference is to get away from my desk and do something non-writerly and non-tech, like washing the breakfast dishes or playing with the cat, but it's entirely up to you. Just be back at your desk in five minutes time, all right?

Carving out some *you* time

However you choose to work, try to make it regular. An hour every week-day is better than five hours at the weekend for two reasons. First, weekends are goof-off times. It's harder to get motivated, and if someone suggests some fun activity or a couple of days away, you've just blown that week's writing. Second, it's more efficient. Doing it daily keeps the story ticking over in the back of your mind. You won't find yourself sitting down and thinking, "Where did I get up to last week ...?")

Now you know how much leisure time you have each week and where it goes, carve out a regular slot each day for writing. Aim for an hour and try to write 300 words in that time. (How much is 300 words? Six times this paragraph, which measures 50 words.)

Three hundred words may sound a lot, but it's only five words a minute. That's one word every 12 seconds. You can do that, surely? Try speaking at the rate of one word every 12 seconds. Sheesh![6]

And if you can't do a full hour in a single sitting, break it down. Aim for 150 words in 30 minutes, 75 words in 15 minutes, or even 25 words in five minutes. Why? Because the numbers soon start adding up. Check it out ...

```
       300 words x 5 days a week
          = 1,500 words a week

        1,500 words x 52 weeks
        = 78,000 words in a year
```

The average novella is 30-40,000 words. The average novel is 70-80,000 words. That's two novellas or one novel in a year. In less time than you now spend watching ads on television.

So get writing!

Key points from this chapter:

- Keep a timesheet to see where your time goes.
- Use systems, not goals.
- Try making intention statements.
- Write with a tomato: try the Pomodoro Technique.

Footnotes:
[1] How humans spend their time: **http://bit.ly/2C15F0K**.
[2] Gym membership statistics: **http://bit.ly/2C4Aq4Y**.
[3] The Pomodoro Technique's web page: **http://pomodorotechnique.com**.
[4] Here's the wind-up timer I use: **http://geoffpalmer.co.nz/htwab02**.
[5] Drafting a book using the Pomodoro Technique: **http://bit.ly/2zY6G9A**.
[6] See Appendix 1 (page 122) for a handy words-per-hour / words-per-minute conversion table.

2: "I'll just check my email ..."

Avoiding Distractions

"You can always find a distraction if you're looking for one."
— *Tom Kite*

We've all been there. Five minutes after settling into a writing session, there's a ping from your email program and you think, "I'll just check that. It won't take a second." The message contains a link to a funny video, so you take a quick look. The video's a riot. You have to share it. Now. It'll only take a moment to pop it on Facebook. You do so, and by the time you've emailed the original sender back to thank them, other friends have responded to your Facebook posting. There's a couple of messages on Messenger too. Might as well check them while you're here. Oh, now there's another email ...

An hour later, you push back from the desk and wonder what happened to your writing time.

The problem: You may be looking at it

If you're reading this on your computer, phone or tablet, you'll know exactly what I mean.

In many ways, computers with word processors are the best writing invention ever. Until quite recently, writers wrote by hand. Imagine *War and Peace* written out in longhand. Or Dickens' *A Tale of*

Two Cities. Now imagine being the printer, setting out each line of type, letter by letter, while trying to read some barely decipherable scrawl ...

A lot later, typewriters came along, which simplified the process to a degree.[1] The scratching of a nib was replaced by a mechanical clackety-clack and the end of each line was prefaced by warning bell, at which point the writer hit a lever to advance the paper a few millimetres and physically throw the carriage back to its starting point. (The origin, by the way, of that obtuse term Carriage Return.)

There were still problems with typewriters. Making corrections was awkward. So was making copies. In the days before photocopiers, carbon paper was the only way to go; tissue-thin stuff that you interleaved between pages. If you struck each key firmly enough, you could get three or even four copies simultaneously, although readability disappeared rapidly with depth, and just handling the stuff left you looking like you'd been fingerprinted by the police.

Word processors emerged in the 1960s as an offshoot of the computer revolution. (The term "word processing" was one of the New York Times hip buzz words for 1971.) And they really were a revolution. You could cut and paste paragraphs without a glue pot, move things around without having to renumber all your pages, and even search and replace text. No more needing to sit down and retype the whole thing to produce a clean copy because you always had it on file and could print out a pristine draft (on your dot-matrix printer, of course) any time you liked.

It was pretty damn good, actually. Not perfect, but close.

Headings, different fonts, centring text, italicising, page numbering and so on required the use of arcane commands and control characters that just had to be learned. Screens were green, you see, with 80 or 132 fixed-width characters per line, so you were never really sure you'd got everything right until you did a printout.

Then along came GUIs (Graphical User Interfaces) with WYSIWYG (What You See Is What You Get) displays. What's on screen is exactly what you'll see on the printed page, which is pretty bloody fantastic when you think about it, but it also leads to a subtle problem I'll mention shortly. For now, there's another, bigger one. A huge one, in fact.

The elephant in the room

Don't get me wrong, I couldn't live without a word processor. In school, my handwriting was so bad that I took up printing, and in high school I typed all my assignments and essays – two-fingered on a clackety old Olivetti – because if I wrote them out longhand even I would struggle to read them a week later.

When home computers emerged, I was there. My first proper computer was the magnificent BBC Micro. 32KB RAM, a full-size keyboard and a 5¼ inch floppy disk drive for storage. The word processor came on a ROM chip that plugged into the motherboard and you started it with the command: *WORD. That was it. The computer was now a word processor, nothing more. You couldn't switch backwards and forwards and play games or use it for anything else. Bliss!

If Dickens or Dostoevsky wanted to check the latest news or tomorrow's weather, they'd have to send out for a copy of the newspaper. All we have to do is Alt-Tab (or Cmd-Tab if you're on a Mac) and flick to another window. So easy. And horribly distracting!

For years now, computers have been so powerful they can run multiple applications at once. You can design a book cover, play music, track breaking news, keep an eye on your email and social media accounts, all while working on your next (or first) novel. Amazing!

Or perhaps not.

Have you ever walked into a room intent on doing something, then forgotten what it was when you got there? It's a common experience – it's called the Doorway Effect – and has a simple, evolutionary explanation. To our brains, changing rooms is equivalent to a sudden change in our environment, and that causes our attention to be reset at a deep, subconscious level. (Are there any threats here? Food sources? Friends or foes?) Our previous mental state is overridden for a few tenths of a second as we take in the environmental change.

And guess what? You don't need to change rooms to suffer the Doorway Effect. Just doing an Alt-Tab (or a Cmd-Tab) will do it.

The myth of multitasking

Research dating back as far as 1927 shows that human beings are rubbish at doing more than one or two things at once. Oh sure, we can all walk and chew gum at the same time, even hold a conversation too, but any real brain work – stuff that requires careful thought and concentration – requires focus. Each time you swap tasks on your computer, your brain does a sort of mini reset, and while each reset may only take a fraction of a second, it can add up to a 40% loss of efficiency. And that's just doing mundane office tasks, not the particular focus and concentration that writing demands.

> *"Although switch costs may be relatively small, sometimes just a few tenths of a second per switch, they can add up to large amounts when people switch repeatedly back and forth between tasks. Thus, multitasking may seem efficient on the surface but may actually take more time in the end and involve more error ... even brief mental blocks created by shifting between tasks can cost as much as 40 percent of someone's productive time."*[2]

People who claim to be good at multitasking are really just fooling themselves. All they're actually doing is several things at once, poorly.

> *"Perceptions of the ability to multitask were found to be badly inflated; in fact, the majority of participants judged themselves to be above average in the ability to multitask. These estimations had little grounding in reality as perceived multitasking ability was not significantly correlated with actual multitasking ability as measured ... Thus, it appears that the persons who are most likely to multitask ... are those*

with the most inflated views of their abilities."[3]

Think about that next time your email program pings to say you've got a message, or you flip over to check Facebook, or send a quick text on your phone.

The solution's simple and obvious. Turn off your phone, (or mute it and toss it in a drawer), then shut down everything on your computer except for the word processor. Set your timer for a pomodoro-period and get to work. Easy. But sometimes people struggle with doing that and need a little outside help.

Software solutions

A friend in the hardware business reckons there's no hardware problem that can't be solved by buying more hardware. (Well, he would say that.) In the same vein, if you really don't have the willpower to keep away from other programs when you should be writing, you might consider installing another program.

As the name suggests, blockers block internet access – and even access to other programs – for a fixed period of time. Here's a few you might like to consider:

> **Cold Turkey** (for Windows and Mac)
> **http://getcoldturkey.com**
> The free version has a timer and blocks websites. The paid version, (a one-time payment), also blocks applications. You might like to bundle it with Cold Turkey Writer Pro which lets you set a minimum word count or work time and won't quit until you're done.

> **Freedom** (for iPhone, iPad, Mac, and Windows)
> **http://freedom.to**
> An internet, app and website blocker. Has a free 7-use trial.

Thereafter it's a modest monthly fee.

Anti-Social (for Windows and Mac)
http://antisocial.80pct.com
A slightly more focused blocker, Anti-Social only blocks websites that make you unproductive. Start it up and you won't be able to access Twitter, Facebook, Flickr, Digg, Reddit, YouTube, Hulu, Vimeo, or any standard web email programs. It's fully customisable, comes at a fixed price, and a trial version is available.

Personally, I don't use any of these programs, but I know of people who do and swear by them. Whatever works for you …

Hardware solutions

What about buying a dedicated computer or laptop just for your writing? Seriously. You don't need anything particularly modern, whizbang or stylish, or even spend much money. I've yet to come across a word processor – even the one on my old BBC Micro – that can't keep up with my sluggish typing speed, and if you don't connect it to the internet, so much the better.

The machine I'm writing on at the moment is an elderly Dell office PC that I picked up at auction for $25. It's running Linux, the free operating system, and LibreOffice, the free open source office application that comes with most Linux installations. (LibreOffice is also available for Mac and Windows, also free, meaning you can have a common application on all your machines. Visit **http://libreoffice.org** to download it.)

I won't get too technical here – it's beyond the scope of this book – but you'll find Linux CD/DVDs included as cover disks on many Linux magazines, or you can download and burn a disk yourself. Personally, I recommend the Ubuntu distribution (**http://ubuntu.com/desktop**).

Two words of warning: Your old machine will almost certainly come with an old version of Windows. Linux will happily co-exist with it, and you can choose which operating system to run at boot time, but be careful with old versions of Windows, *especially* Windows XP. If you connect XP to the internet, you're connecting up a virus magnet.[4] You're much better, and safer, sticking with Linux.

The other caution is to make sure you do regular backups. Older hardware may not be as reliable as brand new gear, but even that's no guarantee. I've had new hard disk drives die after two hours, and whole systems die after two weeks.

If you've got the money and fancy a stylish, dedicated, distraction-free word processor – actually billed at the world's first smart typewriter – you might like to check out the Freewrite. Visit **http://getfreewrite.com**.

The sneakiest distraction of all

Early on in this chapter, I hinted at another subtle problem with working on a computer. Let's address it now because it can be a killer. These are perhaps the sneakiest of all distractions because of the way they come dressed: they're always quite definitely writing-related.

Let me give you an example ...

This morning, working on another project, (an historical novel), I used the term "pickpocket" and a question immediately sprang to mind: Would Victorians have used that word? *Look it up. It won't take a second, honest ...*

I resisted. I know the cunning ways of such distractions now, and I know how to deal with them. I simply followed the term with two question marks, like this: *"It might have been a pickpocket??" she said.* Then I carried on. Those double question marks are an easily-searchable indication for things I need to check later – *outside* of my writing time.

Why is this important? Because writing-related distractions are rabbit holes you can fall down and lose yourself in without even noticing. At least until you come to your senses, sometimes hours later, wondering why you're running late for work. Oh, you've been splendidly entertained. Engrossed, even. And you're wiser too. *But you've got nothing done!*

I can't tell you how many times I've fallen into this sneaky trap.

Before computers, checking something like the etymology of the word *pickpocket* would have required a note on a pad followed sometime later by a trip to the library. Now all that's required is a trip to the search engine. It's deadly! And subtle!

(Should the preceding be one or two sentences? Should "multitask" be hyphenated? What does the *Chicago Manual of Style* have to say about exclamation marks …?)

The need to verify things and to do research (which we'll address in Chapter 4) can be pernicious and crippling. It even sneaks into things like finding names for your characters. In my novel *Payback*, which opens with this line:

> *Solikha Duong was nine years old when she killed two men.*

Solikha was originally just "aa". I needed a Cambodian name, but I also needed to get on with a story that was unfolding as I typed. So I made up something that was easily searchable, and carried on. Later, in non-writing time, I did some research over a glass of wine and came up with a particularly apt name – which you'll discover if you read the book[5] – then did a quick find-and-replace.

I can't stress how important this is, or how subtle it can be. Anything that threatens to break you out of your creative, story-telling state *must* be resisted. Leave it till later when you're in a different frame of mind, because only writing is writing.

A footnote

I later discover (via Online Etymology[6]) that the word "pickpocket" dates back to the 1590s, became a verb in the 1670s, and had its origins in the term "pick-purse" from the late fourteenth century. Fascinating stuff. Very distraction-worthy. But it's not actually writing.

A footnote to the footnote

In the end, I didn't use it. I cut that scene from the final novel.

The baby elephant in the room

There's one other writing distraction I haven't covered yet, and it's equally insidious. It comes under the term of *futzing*, and your computer actually encourages it. Changing the background, realigning your desktop icons, changing your preferences or colour scheme; it's all futzing. Messing around. Time-wasting dithering that can really seem important but actually isn't.

You can even do it inside your word processor. *Should that font be sans or serif? Would chapter headings be better at 14pt? I wonder what this option does …?*

And turn off spelling and grammar checking as you type. It only on encourages another sort of futzing. *Did I mean to use the passive voice there? OMG, there are sentence fragments all over the place!* I leave spell-checking to the very end of a story or book. It's a sort of reward; a mark of completion. And I *never* use the grammar checker. *I'm* in charge of this text, not some anonymous programmer.

Stopping the distraction attraction

If you want to send and receive emails, fine, do that. Browse the web? Go right ahead. Play a quick game of Solitaire? No problem. But if you want to write, properly and well, shut everything off but your word processor. Hell, even disconnect from the internet if you really can't trust yourself not to take a peek at Twitter or Facebook. And shut off your mobile phone too. If you're really so important that you absolutely *have* to be available 24/7, maybe you should focus on that role and come back to writing later.

Seriously, will the world stop turning if you can't be reached for an hour?

Yes, I know, it's simple in theory but difficult in practice. Some people find it almost impossible, at least to begin with. All I can suggest is you start small. Pomodoro slices of 25 minutes followed by a five-minute distraction-blitz, then back to work. In time, you'll come to relish being distraction free. And you'll also see a marked increase in your daily word count.

Remember, only writing is writing.

Key points from this chapter:

- Become aware of distractions, both external ones – such message-received beeps from your phone – and internal ones – such as spelling and grammar checking, or simply playing around with the look of your PC when you should be writing.
- While you're writing, shut off external distractions. That includes your phone, email, internet browser, etc.
- Avoid multitasking. Writing requires focus and concentration.

Footnotes:

[1] Apparently, J R R Tolkien typed all 1,200 pages of *The Lord of the Rings* on a manual typewriter using only two fingers. That must have been Mordor. (Sorry!)

[2] *Multitasking: Switching Costs*, American Psychological Association. **http://www.apa.org/research/action/multitask.aspx**.

[3] *Who Multi-Tasks and Why? Multi-Tasking Ability, Perceived Multi-Tasking Ability, Impulsivity, and Sensation Seeking*, Sanbonmatsu, Strayer, Medeiros-Ward, and Watson. **http://journals.plos.org/plosone/article?id=10.1371/journal.pone.0054402**.

[4] Seriously! Check this link: **http://www.wired.com/2017/05/still-use-windows-xp-prepare-worst**.

[5] *Payback*, by Geoff Palmer is available here: **http://geoffpalmer.co.nz/htwab03**.

[6] Online Etymology: **http://www.etymonline.com**.

3: "My mind's a blank."

Dealing with the Empty Page

*"You can't wait for inspiration.
You have to go after it with a club."
— Jack London*

Perhaps the most common question writers get asked is, "Where do you get your ideas from?" The answer's simple: we invoke the Idea Pixie, say the words, "A new plot, please," accompany the request with a secret incantation, and *abracadabra*, a new plot appears, neat, complete and ready to go.

Actually, it's not like that at all.

There's no such thing as the Idea Pixie.

She's really a *fairy* ...

No writer I know (or have read about) has ever said their plots come to them perfectly formed, complete with characters, locations, a whodunnit and an ending – happy or sad. It doesn't work that way, and I'm delighted it doesn't because half the fun of writing is exploring and discovering *what* you're writing about. When characters come alive in your mind and hit you with a memory or an experience that's shaped them, or when they don't do what you were expecting and head off in another direction entirely, that's the *wow* of writing. It can be disconcerting, but it's also tremendous fun. And just think, if the characters come alive so vividly in your mind – and you're the writer – how do you think your readers are going to feel about them?

Plotters vs pantsers

It's often said that writers come in two forms, plotters or pantsers. They either sit down beforehand and work out every detail of the story, planning it out like an army march then heading out and never deviating from the pre-planned route, or they sit at a blank screen and simply write whatever comes into their heads – in essence, writing *by the seat of their pants*.

In truth, most of us are a mix of the two. I've written several novels with no more preparation than the thought, "Tomorrow, I'm going to start a new novel", but there often comes a point where I need to scribble down some ideas, thoughts for future expansion or development. I rarely use all of them, but *the writing itself generates ideas*. (Read the last part of that last sentence again. If there's any real secret to this game, it's the bit I put in italics.)

Ian Rankin apparently sits at his keyboard, says, "I wonder what Inspector Rebus is up to today?" and starts writing. But he's a tremendously experienced author with more than forty novels under his belt. Lee Child too begins without any prior planning and writes only one draft, but if you read Andy Martin's book[1] about the writing of *Make Me*, (Martin sat behind Child and watched him work), you'll see a constant backward and forward process of revisions, tweaks and changes. (Right near the end, Child even changes the name of one of the book's main characters.) It takes him around six months to write a new Jack Reacher, starting, by habit, on 1 September and finishing in March, but what seems clear is that at least part of the rest of his time is spent filtering through possible ideas in a near-subconscious process.

A practical example

What do I mean by *the writing itself generates ideas*? Let me take you through an idea I had over lunch one day, and how it became a series of five novels.

I was microwaving a snack and thinking about how the book I was revising still wasn't working, despite many rewrites. "I need a break," I decided. "Something light-hearted, fun and exciting." Distracted, I punched in one too many zeros on the microwave's timer, not realising I'd done so till my snack was happily revolving. Rather than reset it, I just waited it out and hit the door release after two minutes. I didn't time it exactly, the microwave's clock showed 17:56, and a thought occurred to me: wouldn't it be neat if I could save up that extra time? Imagine, having lunch with a friend. You're deep in an amazing conversation, then she glances at her watch and says, "Oh no, I've got to get back to work." "Hold on," you tell her, "I have an extra 17 minutes and 56 seconds here ..."

Silly idea, right? But kind of fun.

I started to think more about it. We don't have this technology (yet), but aliens might. How would they use it? How would human beings get involved?

That afternoon I started writing, tentatively at first, the story of a boy who does exactly what I'd done at lunchtime. Tim Townsend mistypes the time into an old microwave and ruins the after-school snack his aunt left out for him and his sister, Coral. He stabs at the door release, unleashing a cloud of smoke and leaving time on the microwave's clock. As he coughs and waves it aside, he spots a couple of mice on a high shelf in the kitchen studying the reading on what looks like a tiny calculator. They look up, high-five each other, then do a little victory dance, like they've just found exactly what they were looking for. "What the heck ...?" Tim thinks.

And so it began. Just that snippet threw up more questions and a lot more ideas. Who are Tim and Coral and what are they doing at their aunt and uncle's remote farm? Who are the mice? (Aliens, obviously, taking mouse forms, but why?) And what's with that old microwave? At one point the mice need to communicate with Tim, and do so, but how could they? Mice, even super-intelligent ones, can't form words, and this ain't Disney ...

The more I wrote and worked out solutions, the more ideas and questions popped into my mind. I started a parallel document – part synopsis, part idea dump, part *aide mémoire*. ("Remember to explain why X did Y."). Characters popped up too. They'd throw up obstacles and I'd have to find a way for my heroes to get around them. It was tremendous fun. Even partway through the book I knew I'd have no room to fit it all in so I started thinking about a sequel. (The first book in that series is called *Too Many Zeros*[2] and was originally published by Penguin.)

When I was done, one of my early readers – who loved it from start to finish – said, "How on earth did you think of all that?" The truth is, I didn't. Not all at once. But one idea led to another. It's an evolutionary process, not a single moment of inspiration.

> "I don't make plots in advance. I ... try to throw people into a messy life and see how they'll sort it out while I'm writing. So the whole adventure is one I share with the reader."
> — John le Carré

The seven basic plots

There are supposed to be just seven basic plots, at least according to Christopher Booker, who reckons he studied the subject for 34 years. He detailed them all in his 2004 book, *The Seven Basic Plots: Why We Tell Stories*,[3] but here they are in brief.

- **Overcoming the Monster:** The lead character learns of a threat or a great evil and sets out to destroy it. Example: *The War of the Worlds*, by H G Wells.
- **Rags to Riches:** The poor, downtrodden lead character battles adversity and ridicule, finally overcoming it all, finding success, wealth and the perfect mate. Eg: *Jane Eyre*, by Charlotte Brontë.
- **The Quest:** The lead character, often accompanied by companions, desperately needs to get somewhere or acquire a particular object. Difficulties and dangers ensue. Example: *The*

Lord of the Rings, by J R R Tolkien.

- **Voyage and Return:** The lead character goes to a strange place, overcomes whatever's thrown at them and returns, richer for the experience. Example: *Alice in Wonderland,* by Lewis Carroll.
- **Comedy:** A poorly chosen category title, this doesn't just refer to humour, more a certain lightness of tone and a happy ending. The key theme is triumph over adversity. Most romances, therefore, fall into this category. Example: *Bridget Jones's Diary,* by Helen Fielding.
- **Tragedy:** The lead character has a flaw, a weakness, or makes a terrible mistake that ultimately leads to their downfall, and possibly those around them. Example: *Macbeth,* by William Shakespeare.
- **Rebirth**: During the course of the story, something happens to the lead character, forcing them to change their ways and become a better person. Example: *A Christmas Carol,* by Charles Dickens.

The reason I mention them is that they're often quoted in writing classes and how-to books, but personally I don't find the breakdown helpful. The categories are interesting at an analytical level, and it's fun to work out where a favourite book or film fits in the list, but from a writing perspective they're useless. I may be wrong, but I really don't think Charlotte Brontë took up her pen one day saying, "I think I'll try a Rags to Riches story." Nor did Charles Dickens go, "Hmm, perhaps a Rebirth tale this time ..." So where *did* they start?

> "However many characters may appear in a story, its real concern is with just one: its hero or heroine. It is he with whose fate we identify ..."

That was Booker, and that pretty much nails it – at least from a writer's perspective.

Even if Brontë and Dickens did start out as coldly and deliberately as I've suggested, *Jane Eyre* and *A Christmas Carol* are way more than simple plot lines. They're about characters, real people, "with whose fate we identify".

Characters and situations

There's an old saying that "character is action", and it's true to a degree, but there's a little more to it than just character, which is why I've headed this section characters *and* situations.

Ebenezer Scrooge is a mean old man who hates Christmas, but his *situation* is one in which he can do real harm (or good). Harry Potter is a boy wizard, but his *situation* is that he's a rather exceptional one. It's the combination of these elements – and many others – that make them engaging stories.

Most people's favourite subject is themselves. Their second favourite subject is other people. They love watching them, talking about them, and reading about them and the situations in which they find themselves. Whether it's "[FAMOUS ACTOR'S] TUG-OF-LOVE BABY" or Jane Eyre's loveless childhood, a character and their situation is immediately interesting.

Typical advice to beginner writers is to (1) decide on a plot and (2) add characters, as if it's some sort of recipe. Many even advise using cookbook-type character sheets. I have one in front of me. Take a look:

```
Name:
Character Type:
Connection to Lead:
Story Goal:
Gender:
Age:
Appearance:
```

```
            Height:
            Body Type:
            Hair Colour:
            Eye Colour:
        Mannerisms:
        Distinctive Speech Patterns:
        Personality:
        Background:
        Personal Life:
        Private Life:
        Work Life:
        Strengths:
        Weaknesses:
```

In reality, I don't know of anyone who works like that – except for the people giving writing advice – but if this sort of breakdown helps get your creative juices flowing, embrace it. There are no right ways and wrong ways in this. Use whatever works for you. And by the same token, discard whatever doesn't. Don't force yourself into a straitjacket methodology because someone tells you, "This is the way it's done." There are no "correct" ways of writing a book, just what works for *you*.

Weaving a story

To my mind, there are two ways of working. There's what I call the "editor-writer" – the analytical me that keeps an eye on spelling and punctuation, logical flow, character consistency, plot points and all the mechanical aspects of the plot – and the "instinctive-writer" – the creative me who loses himself in the story. The eternal battle is to shove that first guy aside and let the second guy have a turn at the keyboard because that's where the magic really starts.

There's an old expression that talks of *weaving a story*. It's a delightful metaphor because that's exactly what it's like; taking a thread of character, a thread of plot, a thread of situation, a thread of action and working them into a tapestry. The danger of breakdowns like Booker's seven plots or character sheets like the one above is that they lead neophyte writers into thinking that's the way the pros work, when it's actually the opposite. It's not a mechanical process, it's a more holistic one.

Easy for me to say, right? But how do you actually go about it? Simple. By asking the age-old questions: who, what, when, where, why and how.

Remember the idea that triggered *Too Many Zeros*: storing time so you could use it later? It was just that, a silly idea, until I started asking questions. Who would do such a thing? Why? Where is this taking place? Who finds out? Why do they need help? What happens next? Many answers triggered more questions that led me deeper and deeper into the story.

Award-winning English novelist John Fowles lived in Lyme Regis, a town on the Dorset coast famed for fossils and a harbour wall known as The Cobb. In a half-dreaming state one morning, Fowles had a vision of a woman standing on that sea wall during a violent storm. Her back was to him, but her clothes appeared to be Victorian. Who was she? he wondered. What was she doing there?

That vision and those questions provided the seed for his novel *The French Lieutenant's Woman*, (and the Academy Award-winning film that was based on it). Just that glimpse. And those questions. The story, and the meta-story within it, emerged as he wrote it.[4]

Which brings me back to where I began this chapter. You don't need One Big Idea before you can start writing a book. You just need to start. And ask questions. The plot and the characters will begin to emerge of their own accord, guided, now and then, by your own judgement and experience. Sometimes this happens quickly, sometimes it takes a while, but the only way to make it happen is to keep working away at it.

Key points from this chapter:

- Are you a plotter or a pantser? Try mixing both!
- It's reckoned there are really only seven basic plots. What makes each story unique are the characters, how they interact, and situations in which they find themselves.
- Some writers use character checklists to get their ideas flowing. Have *you* tried them?
- The act of writing actually generates ideas. So just start writing!

Footnotes:

[1] *Reacher Said Nothing: Lee Child and the Making of Make Me*, by Andy Martin, available here: **http://geoffpalmer.co.nz/htwab01**.
[2] You'll find *Too Many Zeros* here: **http://geoffpalmer.co.nz/htwab04**.
[3] *The Seven Basic Plots: Why We Tell Stories*, by Christopher Booker, available here: **http://geoffpalmer.co.nz/htwab05**.
[4] You'll find a description of this process in *Notes on an Unfinished Novel* by John Fowles, found in *The Novel Today*, edited by Malcolm Bradbury, available here: **http://geoffpalmer.co.nz/htwab06**.

4: "I don't know anything about ..."

How Much Research Do I Need?

"Every writer I know has trouble writing."
— Joseph Heller

The need for research is a doozy of an excuse for two reasons; it *feels* like writing, and it's scope is almost infinite. You can expand it any direction, from developing your story's background and characters, to working out the intricacies of the plot. If the action takes place in a fictional town, you need to build a town – give it some history, geography, a climate. If it takes place in a real one, one you've never seen before, no worries. We've got some fantastic tools these days. Check it out on Google Maps, zoom in and move about the place in Street View. Hey, *there's a coffee shop I can use. And the getaway car could be parked in that alley. Boy, readers are going to love my accuracy and detail.*

Or perhaps not. But don't listen to me.

Listen to Lee Child

A couple of years ago, thanks to a Goodreads promotion,[1] I got to ask Lee Child – the best-selling, one-draft writer we first met in the Introduction as Jim Grant – how he fits in research. Here's my question and his response:

> **Geoff Palmer:**
> I'm interested in your writing process. You've said elsewhere that the final book is pretty much your first draft; that you sit down, start writing and see where the story leads – both you and Reacher. But what about research? A lot of your books contain detailed descriptions of places, weapons, etc. Do you incorporate that as you go? Or do you add these details in later, once you've got the story sorted out?
>
> **Lee Child:**
> You could say a writer's whole life is research. Everyone I meet, everything I read or see or experience is packed away for future use. Whether to do extensive research to ensure all your facts line up is an interesting question. When writing fiction, I don't think accuracy matters as much as whether people perceive accuracy. If I wrote a novel set in New York City, I could make it extremely accurate, but my guess is the more accurate I made it, the more people might find it inaccurate. What matters is not what NYC is really like, but what people generally think it's like. Readers will sometimes mail me to correct mistakes they've found in my books and sometimes they're right, but surprisingly it's usually the things I research most carefully that they say I got wrong. All in all, if you're convincing rather than accurate, you'll probably please more readers.

Fiction vs non-fiction

At this point, writers of non-fiction will be shaking their heads while gesturing to the stacks of notes they've accumulated and all the gaps still unfilled. *It's okay for you guys ...* And it is. You're right, carry on. But let's be clear: research isn't writing. Working up backgrounds, plotting, character development, story arcs ... none of it is writing. All that ultimately counts is the words in your book, not the words your readers will never see, which is why I'm going to say this in a centred, italicised, bold font:

Only writing is writing!

No one's immune. That Lee Child quote above? I almost zipped over to Goodreads to look it up. (*It won't take a second. Do you remember it quite right? Will it really fit there, or does it need more of an introduction ...?*)

But this is my *writing* time. Writing time is a separate beast from research time, so for now the what-will-be-a-Lee-Child quote reads: *?? Lee C on Goodreads*. (Remember that double-question mark? I told you about it in Chapter 2. I use it as an easily-searchable placeholder for things I'll check, correct or add later – in my *non-writing* time.)

At some point you need to finish with research, (or backgrounding, or plotting, or character development), and start working on what readers will eventually see; the finished text. There'll still be gaps. You can't think of everything beforehand. You'll still hit Lee Child moments like I did above. But don't let them interrupt your flow. Add a placeholder and perhaps a note so you can sort it out later, then press on. Because only writing is writing.

Makers of other worlds

Certain fictional genres often require the construction of whole other worlds. Distant planets, perhaps. Alien species. Or an alternate Earth where magic and mystery reign supreme. Historical fiction too may require a mix of hard research and what's called world-building – creating imagined places that feel solid, consistent and real to the reader.

I'm a fan of the galaxy-spanning works of Peter F Hamilton and

Kevin J Anderson who produce fat doorstops of books featuring dozens of characters on multiple worlds. Hamilton's *Night's Dawn Trilogy*, for example, runs to 1.2 million words. Obviously, the characters, planets and the sequence of events he charts need consistency and careful planning. (The last dozen pages of my copy of *The Neutronium Alchemist* are occupied by a timeline and a cast of characters, ships, habitats and planets.) So surely world-building qualifies as writing?

Nope. Only words on the page – the story itself, what the reader will read – actually count.

This might seem unnecessarily harsh, but it's too easy to sit back day-dreaming and building a detailed world or backstory – often far more than you'll ever need – and kid yourself you're making progress on *The Book*. You're not. Not really. Only writing is writing.

How much background do you really need?

A few hundred years ago, few people ever left their village. Before railways, the fastest way to way to travel was on horseback, and horses were luxury items most people couldn't afford. Tourism didn't really emerge until the Victorian era, and even then it was only for the privileged few. These days, however, we're all tourists and travellers, even if we've never left home.

Every day, television and movies bring us in fresh views of the world and the people that inhabit it. If I mention a character, snow-blind, battling a fierce storm amidst cliffs of ice and drifting bergs, or another, parched and gasping, reaching the top of a dune to look out over an arid landscape beneath a searing, pitiless sky, there's a good chance you'll immediately form detailed mental images redolent of the Arctic and the Sahara, even if you've never actually visited either place.

But that hasn't always been the case. Someone born and raised on a Pacific atoll (without TV) would need a lot more than "drifting bergs" to put them in the picture. Likewise, one of Dickens' working-class readers would have demanded a bit more than "arid landscape" to give them a feel of the desert. I'm not suggesting you shouldn't describe places, just that the need to do so is less these days because both you and your reader will have similar reference points. Imagine a sunny afternoon in Central Park or cycling across the Golden Gate bridge. What colour's the bridge? What do you see across the park above the tree line? I'm sure your mental images of both are similar to mine, even if you've not visited either city.

It is, of course, a matter of degree and ultimately a creative decision. Place and setting often dictate the mood. Consider this, the opening lines of possibly my favourite Dickens novel, *Our Mutual Friend*:

> "In these times of ours, though concerning the exact year there is no need to be precise, a boat of dirty and disreputable appearance, with two figures in it, floated on the Thames, between Southwark bridge which is of iron, and London Bridge which is of stone, as an autumn evening was closing in."

Would it matter to you, the reader, if Dickens had mixed up his bridges; had said Southwark was stone and London Bridge iron? Some Londoners would have thrown up their hands in dismay at the error, but I'm guessing most wouldn't even have noticed because the background was just that: background. We're already drawn into the story so a few minor details about bridge construction really don't matter. As Lee Child says, "... if you're convincing rather than accurate, you'll probably please more readers."

Putting worlds together

I'm not suggesting research, world-building and backstories are bad ideas. Not at all. Atmosphere is important, and incorporating interesting details can be a great addition to your story, broadening and deepening it while adding layers of interest and illumination. Look at Hilary Mantel's *Wolf Hall* with its brilliant depiction of sixteenth-century England. But background details must be applied with a light touch, not used to batter your readers. There's a temptation to think, "I've done all this work so I'm damn well going to use it," then try to wedge it in, often to the detriment of the story. Keep your cleverness in the background. Let it inform and illuminate, not dominate your tale. And if in doubt, leave it out.

> *"Description must work for its place. It can't be simply ornamental. It usually works best if it has a human element; it is more effective if it comes from an implied viewpoint, rather than from the eye of God. If description is coloured by the viewpoint of the character who is doing the noticing, it becomes, in effect, part of character definition and part of the action."*
>
> — Hilary Mantel

By all means do research and background preparation if you must. Both can provide useful adjuncts and help you immerse yourself in your story. But incorporate it lightly and don't fool yourself you're really writing. Unless it's adding words to the end product, it's not.

Key points from this chapter:

- Research has its place, but don't get bogged down in it. As Lee Child suggests, being convincing rather than accurate will generally please more readers.
- Some stories, particularly in genres such as fantasy and sci-fi, do require world-building, maps, detailed histories, timelines and so on.
- Don't beat your readers over the head with the results of your clever research (or world-building). They're there for a good read, not a lecture.

Footnotes:
[1] Lee Child interviewed on Goodreads: **http://www.goodreads.com/questions/157492**.

5: "I don't think I can do this."

Doubt: Every Writer's Enemy

"A professional writer is an amateur who didn't quit."
— *Richard Bach*

Can I let you in on a secret? My knowledge of English grammar isn't great. Or rather, my knowledge of grammatical terms and definitions. I can tell you the difference between nouns and verbs, (just), I'm less certain about adverbs and adjectives, and when it comes to gerunds, indicatives, conjunctions and predicates ... oh, forget about it.

Does that mean I'm not qualified to be a writer?

The hell it does!

I can *correct* grammar. If you give me a sentence that reads *Who's sweater is that?* I'll correct it to *Whose sweater is that?* Because ... because ... the first one *looks* wrong, okay? I have a good *feel* for language. I know what *sounds* right and makes sense, I just can't tell you all the whys and wherefores.

This can be embarrassing. I've had foreign friends ask, "Is this pronoun indefinite or intensive?" to which my reply is invariably, "Um ... what's a pronoun again?"

"But I thought you have written much books?"

"You mean, 'I thought you have written *many* books.'"

"Why is that better?"

"Er ... Um ... It just is, damn it!"

I grandly think of myself as the writerly equivalent of The Beatles, Jimi Hendrix or Elvis Presley, none of whom could read music. Paul McCartney once said, "I've never practised scales in my life"[1], and do you know what the only class that Elvis failed in high school was? Yep, music.

Yet this idea that you have to have some sort of qualification in order to do practically anything is pervasive. I know of one award-winning author with decades of experience and a dozen novels under her belt who was eased out of teaching writing at a university level because she didn't have a tertiary qualification. (She was replaced by a graduate with no experience, almost nothing published, but with that vital piece of paper – earned, in part, from the displaced tutor's teaching!)

Another (unqualified) writer I know was told by a graduate of a well-known international creative writing course – jokingly, he assured me – that he was "practising without a licence". Yes, yes, very amusing. But it's a bit like racist jokes based on clever word-play; there's still an undertone of disapproval there and a hint of elitism.

Here, in my view, is a thorough, comprehensive and exhaustive list of all the qualities and qualifications you need to become a writer:

- Be a reader.

"Is that it?" I hear you ask.

"Yup."

"You mean reading critical analyses, of course. Discourses on the creative process. The classics. F R Leavis's *The Great Tradition* and—"

"Nope. Just read whatever turns your crank."

Seriously. The best, most comprehensive education you can get about writing is reading stuff. (I assume it's how I've assimilated the rules of grammar.) Not only is it wildly enjoyable, but it's free. There are no lesson plans or lectures, no study requirements, no assignments.

When you're ready to begin writing, you can do so in your own time, at your own pace. And the very best thing is that you can write what you love. Science fiction? Not a problem. Romances? Go right ahead. Kinky sex romps involving werewolves and vampires? Be my guest. A serious novel contrasting the human situation in the early twenty-first century with Puritan settlers in the New World? Fantastic!

You may genuinely crave some sort of writing qualification, but unless it has a real-world value – say, you need it to teach writing – examine your motives carefully. One of the most common excuses I hear is to do with the discipline involved: "I shall *have* to work on my novel. It's a course requirement." But what about afterwards once the course is finished and no one's looking over your shoulder? When it comes to writing, discipline – as I hope you're discovering – is something that comes from within. *You* have to make the time amidst many other competing interests.

Another reason people give for seeking qualifications is that they'll learn about X, Y and Z – as if libraries didn't exist or there was no such thing as internet search.

One *good* thing about qualification programmes – and it applies to writing classes and workshops too – is the collegial atmosphere, meeting and mingling with like-minded people. That can be valuable, but it's still not writing.

If you want to do a writing degree, good for you. Go for it. But ask yourself if you really need it. Or is it just another excuse for putting off making a start on that book you've had in the back of your mind for years?

Another perspective: imagine that instead of doing the course you took a year off anyway and just wrote. How much could you get done in the time you'd spend in class and working on assignments? How many books?

In a 1980 Playboy interview, John Lennon said, "None of us could read music. None of us can write it. But as pure musicians, as inspired humans to make the noise, they [George, Paul and Ringo] are as good as anybody."[2]

If you're a reader, then I bet you can be a writer too.

Writing classes (and other forms of lobotomy)

I've done a few writing classes over the years. Evening sessions; once a week, two hours after work, for six or eight weeks. A better term for them might be writers' support groups because it's doubtful you'll learn anything of value. The singular advantage of them is they'll make you work, producing a short story or a few descriptive paragraphs for next week's session. It's possible to go on doing classes for years, kidding yourself they're providing you with an incentive to write regularly and thus form good habits …

They're not, of course. Quite the reverse. Writing regularly means writing *every day*, not a couple of hundred words on a subject that doesn't interest you. It's invariably short-form stuff too. Short stories or even flash fiction. It has to be if you're to get any sort of feedback. For this, the worst classes will often have each person standing up in turn, reading their deathless prose out loud to their classmates for critique and comments, forgetting that, as a species, writers tend to be more introverted than their peers.

Even in society at large, most people fear speaking in public. I once saw a survey titled Your Greatest Fears that rated public speaking slightly ahead of death! If your turn's coming up, your heart's likely to be beating so hard in anticipation that you can't hear properly, and if you've just been, relief will be washing through your body. In the end, it all comes down to how well it's delivered. I've heard beautiful passages murdered by poor speakers and utter drivel made engaging by good ones.

Writing classes teach other bad habits too. If you're a studious student, you'll work on your 200-300 word assignment all week, finding your Muse and agonising over every fullstop and comma when you really should be bashing it out. (I'll have more to say on this in Chapter

8.) Then comes the rewriting and rewriting and rewriting – known in the business as "turd polishing". It might be shiny, but it's still shit.

The most insidious lesson, however, is the unspoken one. From the first night you'll gauge, often subconsciously, the general interest of the class and end up writing for that audience when you should really be writing for yourself. Let's say the class as a whole is interested in literary short-form fiction but you love rollicking space operas. Oops, bad fit. Even General Fiction types tend to frown on fantasy and romance writers. So you grit your teeth, bury your real voice and try to please the group.

The other nonsense you'll get is little packages of rules presented as ironclad Dos and Don'ts. I can't begin to count how many times I've heard "Only write what you know!" which is clearly rubbish because it immediately precludes using your imagination – surely the whole point of *creative* writing.

In truth, there are no rules. Publishers don't have adverb police hunting down repeat offenders, and you're unlikely to get a visit from the split infinitive patrol if you boldly go on writing the way you do. There are guidelines, certainly, but they're just that: *guidelines*. Take the ones you think relevant and discard the rest.

Rules? You want rules ...?

Back in 1979, New York Times columnist William Safire came up with what he called the *Fumblerules of Grammar*.[3] Here are the top ten:

1. Remember to never split an infinitive.
2. A preposition is something never to end a sentence with.
3. The passive voice should never be used.
4. Avoid run-on sentences they are hard to read.

> 5. Don't use no double negatives.
> 6. Use the semicolon properly, always use it where it is appropriate; and never where it isn't.
> 7. Reserve the apostrophe for it's proper use and omit it when its not needed.
> 8. Do not put statements in the negative form.
> 9. Verbs has to agree with their subjects.
> 10. No sentence fragments.

Writing workshops

While my experience of writing classes has been poor to mediocre at best, writing workshops are another thing entirely. But that's because they're more targeted and generally take place over a weekend or a series of consecutive days. They're often over-subscribed so can be selective about who they accept, and the better ones will ensure all participants are at about the same level and have similar interests. They'll also present a range of speakers so you don't just get one viewpoint. One of the most valuable aspects of them is what happens out of class, during breaks and mealtimes. You'll get a chance to socialise with other writers and share experiences, tips and woes – something that doesn't generally happen in weekly writing classes. Don't underestimate the value of this informal social networking. The participants of one of the three-day workshops I attended some time ago continued to meet regularly for more than two years afterwards.

Not everyone lives in main centres where workshops are typically held, and travel and accommodation can be expensive. Another type of workshop has emerged along with the internet; online ones, often international. At best, they're fantastic. Professionally run by experienced people and targeted to specific areas you'd like to improve. At worst, they can be cons or money-making ventures with exorbitant fees that just regurgitate stuff you'll find online or in your local library.

Many have giveaway titles like "Write a Novel in a Weekend!" or "The Secret of Writing Bestsellers" (penned by someone whose name has never appeared on any bestseller list), and guarantee results in ridiculously short periods of time. There are no secrets to writing, and if there were, if someone stumbled on something truly magical, do you really think they'd sell it? If I discovered some esoteric incantation to guarantee my books became bestsellers, I'd use it to make myself the next J K Rowling or Lee Child. To hell with you lot!

Class checklist

Whether you're looking at a class, a workshop or an online course, here's a few things to keep in mind before parting with your dough:

- **What do you want out of it?** Be specific. If your weakness is characters or dialogue, it's no good doing a scene-setting class.
- **Is it relevant?** There's little point doing a short story workshop if you really want to focus on longer fiction, or vice versa.
- **Who's running it?** Forget their qualifications, what's their writing history? Look up some of their stories or browse their books. Is their writing *your* sort of writing? On a more general note, would you take a class on Getting Published by someone who's never been published and never worked in the publishing industry?
- **Be wary of rash promises and guarantees.** "Learn this secret, and you'll write 50,000 words in a weekend!" That sort of thing.
- **Look at class sizes.** A weekly class of 6-10 people is likely to be more useful than one containing 20-30 people.
- **What do others say about it?** Google it (and the tutor). Ask around on social networks.

What sort of workshops are available?

The choice online is huge. Here's what a quick internet search turned up – and this list is by no means exhaustive.

- Advanced Character and Dialogue
- Author Voice
- Business of Writing, The
- Character Development
- Cliffhangers
- Depth in Writing
- Endings
- How to Edit Your Own Work
- Pacing Your Novel
- Point of View
- Speed
- Teams in Fiction
- Writing and Selling Short Stories
- Writing Fantasy
- Writing Fiction Sales Copy
- Writing Mysteries
- Writing Secondary Plot Lines

The key thing to remember if you do decide to do a course or class is to make sure it addresses a specific need or weakness. It's easy to fool yourself by saying, "It might be useful later." Time away from your desk is time away from writing, and, as you know, only writing is writing.

Key points from this chapter:

- The main qualification a writer needs is to be a reader.
- Consider what you stand to gain by taking a particular class, course or workshop.
- Would you be better off writing than spending all that time in class?

Footnotes:
[1] Paul McCartney interview: **http://www.wingspan.ru/intereng/gp90.html**.
[2] Playboy's John Lennon interview:
http://www.beatlesinterviews.org/db1980.jlpb.beatles.html.
[3] You'll find the full list of "fumblerules" here:
http://www.listsofnote.com/2012/01/fumblerules-of-grammar.html. And there's even a book: **http://geoffpalmer.co.nz/htwab07**.

6: "I'm not in the mood."

Getting in the Zone

*"Show up, show up, show up,
and after a while the muse shows up, too."*
— Isabelle Allende

It's Monday morning, you've had a great weekend, but you're a bit tired. The prospect of a day at work is daunting so you call your boss and say you won't be in today.

"Oh, why not?"

"I don't feel like it."

"Fair enough," she says. "Well, I hope you do feel like coming in again soon. Your job will always be here when you do."

A likely scenario, right? How about this one …?

You arrive home from a grinding day at work knowing you should put in an hour at the keyboard working on *The Book*, but you don't really feel like it.

So you don't.

But I'll make it up tomorrow, you tell yourself.

Hold on, you haven't made up for that lapse last Monday yet.

Well, I'll have a good long catch-up at the weekend then.

But weren't you planning to—?

If it's raining.

Do you see what's going on here?

How often do you do things you don't really feel like doing, yet somehow still get them done? Like work today. Did you really feel like going in? (Really?) And doing the grocery shopping on the way home? And the lawns and laundry at the weekend? And ...? And ...?

Our lives are filled with tasks that just need doing, and we do them without wheedling or making deals with ourselves. So why is it that writing – or any other creative endeavour for that matter – is so much harder to do than something mindless like, say, washing the car?

Stephen Pressfield identified the culprit then named and shamed it in his brilliant little book *The War of Art: Winning the Inner Creative Battle*.[1] He calls it ...

Resistance

> *"There's a secret that real writers know that wannabe writers don't, and the secret is this: It's not the writing part that's hard. What's hard is sitting down to write."*
>
> — *Steven Pressfield*, The War of Art

Pressfield contends that we have two lives:

> *"The life we live, and the unlived life within us. Between the two stands Resistance."*

Resistance is an invisible, implacable force that seems to come from outside ourselves, but it really comes from within.

> *"Resistance cannot be seen, touched, heard, or smelled. But it can be felt. We experience it as an energy field radiating from a work-in-potential. It's a repelling force. It's negative. Its aim is to shove us away, distract us, prevent us from doing our work."*

Attempting *anything* that does not provide instant gratification – whether it be writing, music, painting, dieting, get-fit programmes, education or entrepreneurial activities – will attract Resistance. It's cunning, relentless and takes many forms, (detailed in the book), and the solution is self-awareness, followed by a daily battle.

> *"Someone once asked Somerset Maugham if he wrote on a schedule or only when struck by inspiration. "I write only when inspiration strikes," he replied. "Fortunately it strikes every morning at nine o'clock sharp."*[2]
>
> *In terms of Resistance, Maugham was saying, "I despise Resistance; I will not let it faze me; I will sit down and do my work."*
>
> *Maugham reckoned another, deeper truth: that by performing the mundane physical act of sitting down and starting to work, he set in motion a mysterious but infallible sequence of events that would produce inspiration, as surely as if the goddess had synchronized her watch with his."*

Turning pro

One of Pressfield's suggestions to beating Resistance is to treat your calling the way you treat your job, as if you were a professional, doing all the things professionals do: Turn up every day, on time, stay on the job till it's done, realise you're in it for the long haul, and so on. It sounds simple, but it's very hard to do. And it's a battle that must be fought daily.

> *"... a writer who waits for ideal conditions under which to work will die without putting a word on paper."*
> — E B White

One of the many insidious ways Resistance comes to me is in the title of this chapter; a dull feeling that I'm not really in the mood today. It can take some minutes for my brain to properly engage with whatever I'm working on, and in that start-up time I'm highly suggestible to anything that's *not* writing. (Checking emails, my phone, my website, what's on the news ...) But if I persist, I know from experience the resistance will slip away. In fact, I've almost come to welcome those not-feeling-like-writing times because they often turn out to be my most productive. At the end of an allocated span, I'll invariably carry on, sometimes far longer than planned, sometimes having to tear myself away – which is also great because I know I'll be straight back into it tomorrow.

Production targets

In Chapter 1 I warned about the fallacy of goal setting, arguing that systems are better. Now I'm going to suggest you set goals, *but within the system you've already established.* That difference is important. On their own, goals are woolly things that give no mechanism for how to achieve them, whereas a system sets up a framework in which things can happen. It's the difference between "I'm going to get fit this year" and "On Mondays, Wednesdays, and Fridays I'll run home from work."

Don't do this next bit until you've carved out a slice of time in which to write each day!

Now that you have, set yourself a daily target, say 250 words per hour. Keep a track of the time you spend and the words you write, and see how you go for a week. If you find yourself consistently slaughtering your target, bump it up. The ideal level is to set it slightly above the speed at which you normally work – say, 5-10% more. There are two reasons for this. First, a little pressure will help keep you focused and make you less prone to distractions. Second, you'll push yourself a little harder, meaning you're actively striving to improve. After a while you may find yourself reaching your target comfortably, at which point you can bump it up again. But always do so within reason. A good range is 5-10%. Setting a target that's too extreme can be self-defeating. If you end each writing session feeling a failure, you're less likely to repeat it.

Don't break the chain

Here's a simple trick from comedian Jerry Seinfeld. Every January he'd hang a year-at-a-glance calendar on the wall of his workroom, and every day he wrote some new material he'd draw a big red X over that day. After a few days, a chain of Xs would develop and the idea was that the chain must not be broken. Not only does this give you the satisfaction of marking off successful days, but also a visual reminder to not break the chain.

(In a more advanced form of this you also write up your daily word count too.)

But you don't need to wait until New Year. Start next month. Visit **http://www.timeanddate.com/calendar**, print off your own calendar, and start nuking each day with a big red X.

> *"How to write: Butt in chair. Start each day anywhere. Let yourself do it badly. Just take one passage at a time. Get butt back in chair."*
>
> *— Anne Lamott, Tweet, 25 Jul 2012*

Another trick: at least at the beginning of this process. Scribble down a note about how you're feeling at the start of each session. Just one word such as "keen", "tired", "flat", "blah" etc., then contrast that with how you feel when you fill in your word count/draw your big red X at the end. Within a short period of time, you'll start to notice how little difference those initial feelings have on your actual output; that you can still write even when you don't seem to be "in the mood".

A musing about Muses

Next time someone tells you they're "waiting for the Muse", ask them which one? Most people don't realise there were nine of them. If you want to write a short story, for example, you probably don't want Terpsichore – the muse of dance – turning up.

> The Muses were Greek goddesses of literature, science and the arts, considered to be the sources of all knowledge, and one summoned them, especially before telling a tale. Many ancient works open with such a call, such as this from Homer's *The Odyssey*:
>
> > *"Sing to me of the man, Muse,*
> > *the man of twists and turns*
> > *driven time and again off course,*
> > *once he had plundered*
> > *the hallowed heights of Troy."*
>
> These days, the Muses are associated with artistic inspiration, but their legacy lives on in words like "amuse", "museum" (where they were originally worshipped), "music" and, of course, every time we "muse about" something.

"Discipline allows magic. To be a writer is to be the very best of assassins. You do not sit down and write every day to force the Muse to show up. You get into the habit of writing every day so that when she shows up, you have the maximum chance of catching her, bashing her on the head, and squeezing every last drop out of that bitch."

— Lili St. Crow

Key points from this chapter:

- Be wary of Resistance (with a capital R). It's everywhere and comes in many forms.
- Set yourself a production target such as 300 words a day, or an hour at your writing desk. Put a big red tick on prominently displayed calendar each time you reach your target. Now, don't break that chain of ticks!

Footnotes:

[1] If you only read one of the books I mention in these notes, it should be this one. Seriously. *The War of Art* by Steven Pressfield is available here:
http://geoffpalmer.co.nz/htwab08.

[2] The true derivation of this "nine o'clock" quote is unclear. See
http://quoteinvestigator.com/2013/10/30/inspire-nine.

7: "I don't know where to start."

Writing's Dirty Little Secret

"It begins with a character, usually, and once he stands up on his feet and begins to move, all I can do is trot along behind him with a paper and pencil trying to keep up long enough to put down what he says and does."
— *William Faulkner*

A blank page or screen can be terrifying. It sits staring back at you demanding words, and while your mind is buzzing with ideas, you can't quite seem to find the right ones. What image should you open with? What words? We all know opening lines are critical. All the writing books and blogs say so. They set the tone, grab attention, and how can you possibly match ones like these ...?

> *I was born twice: first, as a baby girl, on a remarkably smogless Detroit day in January of 1960; and then again, as a teenage boy, in an emergency room near Petoskey, Michigan, in August of 1974.*
> — *Jeffrey Eugenides*
> Middlesex

> *I'm still not sure I made the right choice when I told my wife about the bakery attack.*
> — *Haruki Murakami*
> The Second Bakery Attack *(short story)*

It was the afternoon of my eighty-first birthday, and I was in bed with my catamite when Ali announced that the archbishop had come to see me.
— *Anthony Burgess*
Earthly Powers

It was a queer, sultry summer, the summer they electrocuted the Rosenbergs, and I didn't know what I was doing in New York.
— *Sylvia Plath*
The Bell Jar

I was born in 1927, the only child of middle-class parents, both English, and themselves born in the grotesquely elongated shadow, which they never rose sufficiently above history to leave, of that monstrous dwarf Queen Victoria.
— *John Fowles*
The Magus

Many years later, as he faced the firing squad, Colonel Aureliano Buendia was to remember that distant afternoon when his father took him to discover ice.
— *Gabriel Garcia Marquez*
One Hundred Years of Solitude

Or you could start more prosaically:

I'm pretty much fucked.
— *Andy Weir*
The Martian

No, it's not an eloquent opening, but it does the job. It gets the story started. And that's all you're really after.

"*First paragraphs can often be struck out. Are you performing a haka, or just shuffling your feet?"*

— *Hilary Mantel*

Most of us do quite a bit of shuffling to start with, just make sure you keep shuffling forward because I'm about to let you into what – if there is any real secret to writing – you might call the sneakiest, dirtiest one of the lot ...

Ssshh, don't tell anyone this!

Brace yourself. If you're standing up, you might care to sit down. If you're of a nervous disposition or have a medical condition, you may like to have your medication handy. Ready?

While books are read from front to back, they don't need to be *written* that way.

Surprising, isn't it? Possibly even shocking. I may be particularly slow, but it took me years to realise that simple fact. Up until that point, I kept "writing forward" – re-reading what came immediately before then trying to carry it on. If the precursor wasn't quite right it would have to be fixed, then if what came after didn't quite mesh, I'd circle back again in an endless reiterative cycle.

Some of the creative professions can't easily go back and patch up their mistakes. Sculptors, for example. ("Whoops! Well, *this* David didn't have a nose, okay?") Fortunately, writing's not like that.

I've heard of writers starting at the end and working forwards, or working in a piecemeal fashion – a bit here, a bit there – then stitching the patchwork together like a giant story quilt. I had a similar experience myself writing my novel *Telling Stories*. Early on I had a beginning and an end and just needed to fill in the middle bits.

So make a start, any sort of start, and press on. Just get your story down. You can "fancy up" that opening later.

How *do* you get started?

Ah, the $64,000 question. The answer to which is *you just start*.

Take a deep breath. Relax. Clear your thoughts and let out that creative two-year-old hiding away in the back of your mind. It's not important. It's fun. Just let them play and see where they lead you.

What do you see in your mind's eye as you stare at the blank screen or page? Is it a first-person view? (In which case, who are you?) Or a third-person one? (Who is that person?) What's the situation? Where is it? When is it? Look around. What are the sights, sounds and smells? Just *be* in that moment – as yourself or your character – and start to capture it in words. Don't think about plots or endings or character development or any of that other high-school nonsense, just focus on the moment and let it lead you into the next one, then the next one, and the next.

Your creative brain knows how stories work. It's been listening to them since long before you learned to write, and it knows all about that high-school stuff; about beginnings and middles and endings. Just let it go. Set its own pace. See where it carries you.

Don't try to judge or second guess it. You're going along for the ride.

As you travel, you'll find possibilities opening up ahead of you. Ideas, character traits, observations and whole incidents you wouldn't have guessed at seconds earlier appear. It's engaging, enthralling and addictive – which is why we do it.

But it won't happen if you don't make some sort of a start. Even if it's an Andy Weir one.

Another writing secret

The computer age has deprived us of one fascinating resource: first drafts. These days, there's really no such thing. You can still see Dickens' first drafts,[1] every scratch and touch of his pen, every crossing-out and correction, but ours are lost forever in our computer's innards.

That, generally, is a positive thing – although it does make going back and endlessly reworking previous material dangerously easy. The document you start tomorrow, full of fears and trepidation, can be the very same one you send off with a flourish, polished and ready for publication, a year from now. But it shouldn't be.

As I've suggested, in the old days first drafts were tangible items. At the very least you'd need a neat and legible "fair copy" before sending it off to a publisher, (who might then deduct the cost of having it typed up from your future royalties). I suspect this division between the rough and the neat added a subtle but important psychological separation to the writing process, something we've lost in the WYSIWYG world where every keystroke looks as though it's already part of a perfectly finished document. You can even add drop-caps and justify your text, just like in a proper printed book. Why then are we surprised to find ourselves endlessly going back and trying to make everything "just so"?

Stop it, that's all I can say. And you can. The easiest way to do so is to reinstitute the draft. No, not compulsory military service, but a system of working within tangible divisions: rough draft, revised draft and final draft, for example. Because that's writing's other little secret: You can redo stuff and make it better.

Don't start with number one

It may be my computing background, but I never start with Draft 1. I always start with Draft 0 because that's how computer's count. (I should mention I trained as an assembler programmer, and in binary such things are important.)

What difference does it make? A subtle, psychological one, at least to me. Draft 0 is the nothing draft, the throwaway, the one no ever gets to see. It's a place where I can make mistakes, go off on tangents, ramble. The place where nothing matters.

That's not to say it's a cesspit of freewriting, bad spelling and incomplete sentences. I do try to write well, and it does have some structure and form, some coherence. But it's rough around the edges. Workmanlike. The tool marks may still be visible in some places.

Once Draft 0 is complete – and *only* when it's complete – I start on Draft 1. This is where we have one over the write-by-hands and the old-school typists because it's simply a matter of copying the document and renaming it Draft 1. If I've kept a separate document containing a synopsis, notes and ideas, I do the same with that. I then move the original(s) to a folder named Archives in case of a disaster or I ever need to refer back to them, and proceed from there. In a sense, Draft 1 becomes the first real draft because it's semi-presentable and semi-coherent. If I'm lucky, it'll contain large lumps of its ancestor. If I'm not, at least I'll have a framework to work from.

Once Draft 1 is done, I repeat the process and move on to Draft 2.

How many drafts should you do? That's a bit like asking the length of a piece of string; it varies. When you *think* it's done, when you get to the last page, sit back and say, "Yep, that's nailed it," do the following ...

Print it out in full, pop it in a drawer and start on something else. The sequel, perhaps.

In a month or two's time, when the raw heat of creation and the sheer bloody work is a fading memory, pull it out and read it through as if you'd just plucked it from a bookshelf.

This stepping-away period is important. I call it "necessary distance". In the interim, instead of being something you've sweated over for months, *The Book* has now become a thing, an object, something anyone might pick up and read.

So read it!

Mark typos and misspellings by all means, but this is not a critique. You're reading for the story. If your mind wanders or you fall asleep partway through, mark the spot and carry on; you've a bit more work to do there. On the other hand, you may find yourself turning page after page, skipping through the occasional misplaced word or less than perfect sentence because you're caught up in your own story. Perfect! If it's entertaining you, it'll surely entertain readers.

In truth, you'll probably find a mixture of the two, (but hopefully much more of the latter). What *necessary distance* really gives you is some breathing space, some time away from studying the thing through a magnifying glass. You'll see the whole picture more clearly and spot any major weaknesses or misshapen elements.

Then it's decision time. A few quick fix-ups or some heavy-lifting work? A Draft 2.1 or a Draft 3.0? You'll know.

One-draft writers and Heinlein's Third Rule

Some writers contend you should never rewrite, or only do so to "editorial order". It's known as Heinlein's Third Rule and comes from the 1947 book *Of Worlds Beyond: The Science of Science Fiction Writing*, edited by Lloyd Arthur Eshbach. In Heinlein's chapter, the acclaimed sci-fi author wrote:

> *"I'm told that these articles are supposed to be some use to the reader. I have a guilty feeling that all of the above may have been more for my amusement than for your edification. Therefore I shall chuck in as a bonus a group of practical, tested rules, which, if followed meticulously, will prove rewarding to any writer."*

He then proceeded to list his rules:

1. You must write.
1. You must finish what you start.
3. You must refrain from rewriting except to editorial order.
4. You must put it on the market.
5. You must keep it on the market until sold.

A little later he added:

> "The above five rules really have more to do with how to write speculative fiction than anything said above them. But they are amazingly hard to follow—which is why there are so few professional writers and so many aspirants, and which is why I am not afraid to give away the racket! ..."

He's right. They are amazingly hard to follow. And one day I hope to reach his level of focus and proficiency so that I too can get out exactly what I want in a single draft. But it's dangerous advice for newcomers because it doesn't account for where Heinlein was in his career.

Being asked to contribute to a book called *The Science of Science Fiction Writing* is, perhaps, a clue. It seems reasonable to assume that the editor didn't pick a bunch of barely-knowns who'd only had a couple of stories printed in *Astounding Science Fiction*. In fact, in 1940 alone, seven years before this piece appeared, Heinlein wrote three short novels, four novelettes, and seven short stories.[2] A novel he wrote the previous year, (1939), didn't see publication until 2003![3]

In short, these are the words of a man who's conquered his medium. He's been living off his writing for almost a decade. According to a couple of notable critics, "No one ever dominated the science fiction field as Bob did in the first few years of his career."[4]

Rule Three is *not* good advice for beginning writers – or even moderately proficient ones – because it robs them of a key learning facility: the ability to discover and correct their own mistakes. Whether it's the repetition of certain words or phrases, (one of mine is "for a moment"), or gaping plot holes or horrendous character flaws, *not* re-examining your text robs you of a chance to discover the ways in which you work – and sometimes don't. It robs you of a chance to look at your work objectively and, if necessary, fix it.

Rewriting is sometimes conflated with writing a sloppy first draft then going back to fix it. Yes, get the first draft down, but *never* write sloppily; *always* do your best. And sometimes, on reflection, you'll find you could have done better.

Rewriting does *not* mean slavishly changing every sentence just for the sake of it. It simply means finding the bits that don't work, and fixing them.

What's missing from Heinlein's Rules is the *way* in which one-draft writers really operate. The impression given is that they bash out a story in one go and send it off. Write another, send it off. Yes, they may write a story in a single draft, but *within* that draft they're constantly cycling back tweaking it. Need a gun in the penultimate scene? (see Chapter 10), then cycle back and place it in scene one – all within that single draft. In essence, they're writing and rewriting at the same time. It's the result of years of practise and experience, and it's obviously fantastically efficient, but it's unlikely to be something you'll achieve on your first (or even second) novel.

(And presumably, Heinlein put his neophyte 1939 novel "on the market" (Rule #4), and kept it there (Rule #5), even though it didn't "sell" until fifteen years after his death!)

Heinlein's Rules are something to aspire to. A target worth working towards – and I am (slowly!) getting better. But for now, it's still multi-draft me.

> *"Don't get discouraged because there's a lot of mechanical work to writing ... I rewrote the first part of A Farewell to Arms at least fifty times ... The first draft of anything is shit."*
> — *Ernest Hemingway*

Key points from this chapter:

- Just start your story, anywhere, anyhow. You can always tidy and re-order it later.
- Books are read from front to back, but they don't have to be written that way.
- Writing is a form of energy. Words generate more words – if you'll let them.
- Few writers write a perfect first draft.
- Getting a story down is much harder than revising it later.

Footnotes:

[1] Some of them are online here: **http://www.vam.ac.uk/content/articles/t/the-dickens-manuscripts**.
[2] **http://en.wikipedia.org/wiki/Robert_A._Heinlein#Early_work**.
[3] The novel is called *For Us, The Living: A Comedy of Customs*. It's available here: **http://geoffpalmer.co.nz/htwab09**.
[4] Wikipedia, op cit.

Part II

Keeping Going

"Next to the defeated politician, the writer is the most vocal and inventive griper on earth. He sees hardship and unfairness wherever he looks. His agent doesn't love him (enough). The blank sheet of paper is an enemy. The publisher is a cheapskate. The critic is a philistine. The public doesn't understand him. His wife doesn't understand him. The bartender doesn't understand him."

— *Peter Mayle*

8: "This is going nowhere."

Running out of Steam

"Don't get it right, just get it written."
— James Thurber

Marathon runners may hit what's called "The Wall" – sudden, paralysing exhaustion – at around the 28km mark; two-thirds into the gruelling 42km run. The cause is well known – glycogen depletion – and can be avoided or quickly remedied with an energy drink. Writers too often hit a wall of sorts, typically one-third of the way into a new novel. At that point, with the glorious burst of that first flash of inspiration long behind them and the story seeming to grind to a halt, they peer ahead, see the endless hilly miles to come and give up. One-third in is the point at which most novels (and stories) are abandoned.

If you hit the writer's wall, guzzling down an energy drink won't help. The real solution is doing the opposite of what marathon runners do – and almost certainly what your instinct tells you too. You need to speed up.

The cause of the calamity is invariably a toxic mix of self-doubt and uncertainty. Writing can be hard work – not in a physical sense like a road race – but sustained sitting and concentration still take their toll. [1] But it's mostly self-doubt, ("This isn't working any more. What the hell was I thinking?") and uncertainty, ("I don't even know where this is going!")

Like reaching a cliff edge, the natural tendency is to pull back and retrace your steps. You must have taken a wrong turn somewhere. Go back, see if you can spot it.

Wrong!

What you should do it take a running jump. Or rather, a leap of faith.

The cause is our old adversary Resistance from Chapter 6. It's a wily old sod and will use any means it can to slip between you and your creativity.

> "Resistance will tell you anything to keep you from doing your work. It will perjure, fabricate, falsify; seduce, bully, cajole ... It will reason with you like a lawyer or jam a nine-millimetre in your face like a stickup man. Resistance has no conscience. It will pledge anything to get a deal, then double-cross you as soon as your back is turned. If you take Resistance at its word, you deserve everything you get. Resistance is always lying and always full of shit."
>
> — *Steven Pressfield*, The War of Art

Picking up the pace is the way to catch Resistance off guard. Just when it expects you to slow down and start looking around, you put on a burst of speed and leave it in the dust.

It really works! Making yourself go faster focuses your concentration and helps push doubts aside. Ever had an urgent task and a tight deadline? I bet you got it done.

If you typically write 300 words an hour, push for 450. If you do 500 hundred, try for 750. Even if you "fail" and only make 400 (or 650) words, the increased velocity will carry you over the bump and deeper into your story. Once you're back in control, you can carry on at that pace or throttle back. That's up to you. The important – no, the *vital* – thing is to keep moving forward.

Yes, there may well be structural problems somewhere in that first third, but it's only Draft 0, remember? What's easier to work on;

something tangible in black and white, or something that's still unwritten?

The other alternative is to move to a different place in the novel, skip over the bit you're stuck on, and come back to it later. Just because novels are read contiguously it doesn't mean they have to be *written* contiguously.

The myth of slow writing

While we're here, we might as well tackle this head-on: *slow writing does not necessarily mean good writing.*

Like any gathering of creatives, the behind-the-scenes of writing can be a bitchfest. Scratch the surface of any writers' group or organisation and you'll soon find a division between what could be called the *artistes* and all the rest; the view that Literature (with a capital L) is somehow superior to popular fiction such as thrillers, fantasy or romance. It's something Raymond Chandler railed against 70 years ago when he complained of "that snobbism which makes a fourth-rate serious novelist, without style or any real talent, superior by definition to a mystery writer who might have helped recreate a whole literature". (As, indeed, Chandler did. Since his death in 1959, three of his novels[2] have come to be regarded as literary masterpieces.)

Or how about this experience from contemporary science fiction author Neal Stephenson:

> ... a while back, I went to a writers' conference. I was making chitchat with another writer, a critically acclaimed literary novelist who taught at a university. She had never heard of me. After we'd exchanged a bit of small talk, she asked me "And where do you teach?" ...
> I was taken aback. "I don't teach anywhere," I said.
> Her turn to be taken aback. "Then what do you do?"
> "I'm ... a writer," I said. Which admittedly was a stupid thing to say, since she already knew that.
> "Yes, but what do you do?"
> I couldn't think of how to answer the question---I'd

> *already answered it!*
>
> *"You can't make a living out of being a writer, so how do you make money?" she tried.*
>
> *"From ... being a writer," I stammered.*
>
> *At this point she finally got it, and her whole affect changed. She wasn't snobbish about it. But it was obvious that, in her mind, the sort of writer who actually made a living from it was an entirely different creature from the sort she generally associated with.*[3]

Ever wondered why, in most countries, romance writers have their own writers' organisations? Despite the fact that some of their members are the most popular and highest-earning writers on the planet, the genre isn't regarded as being quite respectable. It's not *proper* writing.

Part of this snobbishness seems to derive from the speed of output. Good writing, it's asserted, is like the production of fine wine; it can't be hurried. It takes time. Every word, every nuance is critical, and the true *artiste* constantly hovers between keyboard and thesaurus.

But good things can be done quickly too. Charles Dickens wrote *A Christmas Carol* in six weeks. Longhand. What's more, he wrote it for money. (Sales of his previous book, *Martin Chuzzlewit*, were slowing and his publisher threatened to slash his monthly income.) According to Dickens' biographer, he built the story in his head while taking nightly walks of 15-20 miles, then came home to write it in a "white heat".

Or what about William Faulkner who reckoned he wrote his 1930 classic *As I Lay Dying* from midnight to 4:00 AM over the course of six weeks "and did not change a word of it."[4]

Whether you can run faster or write faster is largely a matter of practise. Regular workouts are essential, as is gently pushing yourself from time to time to build up muscle.

There's another reason to ignore the myth of slow writing: the world has moved on. Once upon a time, publishers believed – without any reason I can discover – that the public could only stomach one book a year from any given author. Which, of course, is nonsense. I first discovered Lee Child two or three years ago and have since read all his books – 21 at the present time. In the same way, TV producers have discovered that viewers like to binge watch their favourite shows, not wait for them to be rationed out at the rate of one a week.

If you read the ripping start of a new fictional series, do you really want to hang around for a year waiting for part two? I have a friend who won't start a Peter F Hamilton sci-fi series until the last book is out, (Hamilton tends to write trilogies), because he likes to blitz through the whole thing in one go.[5]

And from a writer's perspective in this new indie publishing world, getting good books out faster is a sound business move.

Who knows, you might even reach a Nora Roberts (aka J D Robb) level of productivity. Since 1980, she's produced an average of six novels *every single year.*

> "In music we admire musicians who practise ten or more hours a day. Painters and other forms of art are the same. Only in writing does the myth of not practicing to get better come roaring in. We teach new writers to slow down, to not work to get better, to spend fewer and fewer hours at writing, to not practise, and then wonder why so many writers don't make it to a professional level."
>
> — Dean Wesley Smith

Key points from this chapter:

- Slow writing is no guarantee of quality or readability.
- If you find your story's grinding to a halt, skip the place where you're stuck and carry on. You can come back and fix it up later.
- Like many other skills, writing takes practise. So practise!

Footnotes:

[1] Which is why you're taking regular breaks, getting up and moving around as per the Pomodoro Technique in Chapter 1, right?

[2] *Farewell, My Lovely* (1940), *The Little Sister* (1949), *and The Long Goodbye* (1953).

[3] Stephenson's analysis of this division is fascinating and detailed. I summarised here **http://geoffpalmer.co.nz/brief-anecdote-neal-stephenson** and you can read the full thing here: **http://slashdot.org/story/04/10/20/1518217/neal-stephenson-responds-with-wit-and-humor**.

[4] **http://en.wikipedia.org/wiki/As_I_Lay_Dying**.

[5] And Hamilton's book aren't lightweights. His *Night's Dawn* trilogy – which I highly recommend and have read twice – weighs in at around 1.5 million words! The series starts here: **http://geoffpalmer.co.nz/htwab10**.

9: "I just can't go on!"

How to Handle Writer's Block

*"There's no such thing as writer's block. That was invented
by people in California who couldn't write."*
— Terry Pratchett

Writer's block comes in two forms: a general creative slowdown or a complete inability to write. It was first described by psychoanalyst Edmund Bergler in 1947, and well-known sufferers have included F Scott Fitzgerald, the creator of the Peanuts comic strip Charles M Schulz, British songwriter Adele, and it may well have been the reason Herman Melville gave up writing novels shortly after *Moby Dick* was published.

The cause may be external – illness, injury, a family crisis, death of a loved one – in which case you should deal with it exactly the same way as you'd deal with it in your regular job, typically by taking some time off work.

Often, however, the cause is nothing more tangible than "creative difficulties". Common reasons cited include:

- a lack of motivation
- running out of ideas
- too many distractions
- the pressure to produce work

- working against your natural inclination in an unsuitable genre or style
- feeling intimidated by a previous success

Philip Pullman, author of the brilliant *His Dark Materials* series, is less sympathetic:

> "Writer's block ... a lot of howling nonsense would be avoided if, in every sentence containing the word WRITER, that word was taken out and the word PLUMBER substituted; and the result examined for the sense it makes. Do plumbers get plumber's block? What would you think of a plumber who used that as an excuse not to do any work that day?
> The fact is that writing is hard work, and sometimes you don't want to do it, and you can't think of what to write next, and you're fed up with the whole damn business. Do you think plumbers don't feel like that about their work from time to time? Of course there will be days when the stuff is not flowing freely. What you do then is MAKE IT UP. I like the reply of the composer Shostakovich to a student who complained that he couldn't find a theme for his second movement. "Never mind the theme! Just write the movement!" he said.
> Writer's block is a condition that affects amateurs and people who aren't serious about writing. So is the opposite, namely inspiration, which amateurs are also very fond of. Putting it another way: a professional writer is someone who writes just as well when they're not inspired as when they are."[1]

Some years later, when he was asked if he had any tricks or tactics to help get things moving when the words weren't coming out the way he wanted, Pullman replied, "No tricks. I just sit there groaning."[2]

Apart from that, and having someone grab you by the lapels, give you a good shake and shout, "Harden up!" in your face, what else can you do?

Some common suggestions

Here are some ideas to break through the block ...

Freewriting

Spend 5-10 minutes writing anything and everything that comes into your head. Don't worry about whether it makes sense, just get it down as quickly as you can. Some writers do this to limber up at the start of each session. It's the mental equivalent of an athlete's warm-up.

Journaling

Write a diary entry about your day (or, if this is an early-morning session, the day before). This is personal, private and for your eyes only. Like freewriting, the idea is to shove your inner critic aside and get you back into the swing of stringing words together.

Step away from the desk

Personally, I find running useful when I catch myself starting to stew on my own thoughts. There's something refreshing about the switch from mental to physical exertion. Giving your brain what it considers *real* work – "Oh god, a hill!" – frees up the mind remarkably. I've had some of my best ideas and found my way through seemingly intractable plot blocks while out pounding the streets.

> *"If you get stuck, get away from your desk. Take a walk, take a bath, go to sleep, make a pie, draw, listen to music, meditate, exercise; whatever you do, don't just stick there scowling at the problem. But don't make telephone calls or go to a party; if you do, other people's words will pour in where your lost words should be. Open a gap for them, create a space. Be patient."*
>
> — *Hilary Mantel*

Don't go there in the first place

There's a natural tendency to finish a writing session at the end of a chapter, a paragraph, or some other logical block. Instead, try finishing in the middle of ...

That last sentence would be pretty easy to come back to finish off, wouldn't it? And doing so will immediately transport you back into the frame of mind where you left off last time.

> *"The best way is always to stop when you are going good and when you know what will happen next. If you do that every day ... you will never be stuck. Always stop while you are going good and don't think about it or worry about it until you start to write the next day. That way your subconscious will work on it all the time. But if you think about it consciously or worry about it you will kill it and your brain will be tired before you start."*
>
> — Ernest Hemingway

An extreme solution

If you're really stuck, you might like to break the rule of Chapter 2 (Distractions) and try The Most Dangerous Writing App at the website: **http://www.themostdangerouswritingapp.com**.

On arrival, you'll be presented with a Session Length option – which you can set for 3, 5, 10, 20, 30 or 60 minutes – and a Start Writing button. Hit that and you're committed. If you pause for longer than five seconds, you'll see your text dissolve irrecoverably before your eyes. If, however, you make it to the time you've set, you'll be given a chance to

> save your words.
>
> The app claims it's "designed to shut down your inner editor and get you into a state of flow". It certainly does that!

I suspect the prime cause of writer's block is stress, and that results in a self-fulfilling cycle of misery. Procrastinating, and the worthless feelings that result from it, simply add to the burden and wind you up a little tighter. So stop procrastinating. Get something down. Anything. It doesn't matter about the quality. It can always be polished (or discarded) later.

> *"Writer's block is a phony, made up, BS excuse for not doing your work."*
>
> *— Jerry Seinfeld*

Key points from this chapter:

- Writer's block is often just another form of Resistance.
- Freewriting, journaling or taking a walk can help.
- Treat writing like a job. What would your boss say if you claimed to have doctor's block, or bartender's block, or IT consultant's block? Exactly! So get to work!

Footnotes:
[1] **http://www.aerogrammestudio.com/2013/09/16/12-famous-authors-on-writers-block**.
[2] **http://www.philip-pullman.com/qas**.

10: "I need to go back and fix something."

Changer Dangers

"The secret of getting ahead is getting started. The secret of getting started is breaking your complex overwhelming tasks into small manageable tasks, and then starting on the first one."
— Mark Twain

We're moving into dangerous territory here, because the more you get into a story, the more you'll be tempted to go back and change things. Modestly sized things are OK; big and little things are a no-no. But how do you differentiate between modest thing, a big thing and a little thing? That's where it gets tricky.

Lookout, Chekov's got a gun!

Anton Chekov (1860-1904) is considered one of the greatest short story writers in history. He was a stickler for paring down details and removing extraneous information, once famously remarking, "If you say in the first chapter that there is a rifle hanging on the wall, in the second or third chapter it absolutely must go off. If it's not going to be fired, it shouldn't be hanging there." It's advice short story writers in particular might like to note, but its meaning has been twisted over the years, and the term "Chekov's gun" has become shorthand for foreshadowing – the placement of an insignificant object early on that later turns out to be important.

To continue the gun metaphor, let's say your hero, in a desperate situation, gets out of it by snatching a pistol from the top drawer of her desk. *Whoa, hold on a sec. Where did that come from? We didn't even know she owned a gun.*

It's a simple fix: to avoid startling the reader out of the story, you just need a little foreshadowing. Maybe ten chapters earlier she pushes the gun aside in search of a paperclip, and five chapters after that she sees it and thinks how she really must give granddad's old service revolver to a museum. These passing hints of the gun's presence, subtly masked by other establishing detail, make its eventual use much less surprising.

So far, so good. Go back and do a little foreshadowing. Insert the extra lines you need in the appropriate places then *move away from the text!* That's it, keep your hands up where I can see them. Higher. Away from the keys. Now raise your index fingers, and we're gonna do this nice and slow. Place one on the Ctrl key (Cmd if you've got a Mac) and use the other to tap the End key.[1] There, we're back at the end of the document. Easy, huh? Now, as you were. Carry on with your story.

You may not appreciate it, but you've just been saved you from a terrible fate. Something that's ensnared me countless times. The horror of...

Rewriting (and rewriting, and rewriting)

"I can't write five words but that I change seven."
— *Dorothy Parker*

While you were wandering back through your text, fiddling with Chekov's gun and looking for a place to put it, you almost certainly spotted a missing full-stop or some other punctuation glitch, a missing or misspelled word and were tempted to rewrite a sentence or two to clarify them. Little fix-ups like that are OK, but you must never let yourself get dragged into the deeper waters of wholesale changes. As I said at the start, this is dangerous territory because unless you're really careful you'll find yourself rewriting a paragraph, then a section, then a whole chapter, then the whole damn book to finally get back to the point where you simply needed the gun.

What's wrong with that? Simple: the story hasn't moved on. Remember, the aim of every writing session is to keep up the momentum and *move the story on*.

What's more, you've slipped out of creative mode into editing mode. The two are very different. Creative mode is reclusive, quiet and shy, but it's the one that makes your writing zing. The very last thing you want to do is frighten it away before the story's finished!

And what happens when you come to the next "gun" and start doing the same thing? You're creating a bad habit for yourself. *And* adding a huge amount of work. *And*, most likely, squeezing out whatever was fun, original and creative in your story in the first place.

Here's a classic example of how I went back to place a "gun" and ended up shooting a day's output in the head ...

I keep a timesheet and a writing diary, (you can read more about that process in the bonus chapter at the end of this book – under *Treat it Like a Business*), and one notorious incident convinced me of the folly of going back and doing fix-ups. I once managed to produce 17 words in a four-hour session. For the mathematically inclined, that's the heady sum of 4.25 words per hour, or one word every 14 minutes. So much for moving my story on!

I found a couple of sentences that needed tweaking, you see. Then a paragraph, then a description, then a whole chapter. Before I knew it, I was rewriting like a madman – doing second-draft stuff on my first.

It's tempting, horribly, fiendishly tempting, but you have to resist it. Remember that two-finger salute; Ctrl + End (or Cmd + End) to return to the bottom of your text and keep advancing your story.

A writing secret: Gun safety

There's another reason to be wary of Chekov's gun. What if the "gun" in question is something bigger? What if it's a character flaw, or ability, or something you hadn't realised about your lead until this point? Perhaps she's been vehemently anti-guns all through the story. What's this one doing in her drawer? How does she even know how to use it? Now you've got a bit more explaining to do.

(Perhaps her dad was a gun nut. Perhaps he'd drag her off to gun ranges to practise target shooting, something she hated and was hopeless at. But he wasn't all bad. They had fun times together too, and she keeps that old thing in her drawer as a memento ...)

This, obviously, is going to need a lot more work. Not just foreshadowing for the gun, but character foreshadowing too. Whole incidents. Childhood memories. How the hell are you going to handle that?

This is too big, so you're not going to do it right away. You're going to carry on.

I've mentioned before how I work with two parallel documents; the actual story and a synopsis/notepad that also acts as a dumping ground for plot points, ideas and possibilities. A simple note to myself will do it: "Chapter 40. Foreshadow the gun in childhood, background, etc." Then I'll switch back to the text and carry on with the story. Notes like that will be carried to the bottom of the synopsis as the story unfolds, and they'll become the input for any second-draft changes. The natural places to put them will pop out at you on the read-through, and it's not only easier but more efficient than wading back trying to fit them into stuff you wrote weeks or months earlier.

Keep your focus on the finish line. Place the occasional modest-sized "gun" if you must, but be careful you don't blow your writing fingers off.

> "Almost all good writing begins with terrible first efforts. You need to start somewhere. Start by getting something – anything – down on paper. What I've learned to do when I sit

down to work on a shitty first draft is to quiet the voices in my head."

— Anne Lamott

Key points from this chapter:

- Exercise caution going back through your manuscript to make changes, especially on the first draft. Add or delete a line or two by all means, but avoid the temptation to start making corrections or trying to "improve" your prose.
- Getting it down is far more important than making it perfect first time through.
- You can polish prose and plaster over plot holes later, just get it written!

Footnotes:
[1] If you've got a MacBook I'll let you use three fingers. Hit *Cmd + FN + the right arrow.*

Part III

Letting Go

"Writing is a mug's game. It's insanely competitive, appallingly paid, and the only good news about the terrible pay is that the job is so woefully insecure you probably won't have to endure it for long. No one goes into an industry like this to advance a career or pay a heating bill. You go into it for the joy of it, the creative joy. Don't lose that. It's the precious metal from which all else is beaten."

— Harry Bingham

11: "It's still not quite right."

The Pursuit of Perfection

"Ever tried. Ever failed. No matter.
Try again. Fail again. Fail better."
— Samuel Beckett

By this point, you're done. The first drafts are firmly behind you, but the manuscript keeps beckoning you with the song of a siren leading unwary sailors onto rocks. The real title of this chapter should be "I just can't let it go", but of course that's not how it presents itself to you, the writer. In a sense, it's the bedfellow of Chapter 10 ("I need to make some changes"), but it's infinitely more subtle.

By never quite finishing, you're never in the invidious position of having a finished manuscript that you, or anyone else, can sit down and read and coolly assess, for better or worse. On top of that, finishing a manuscript can be like having a death in the family – or a lot of little deaths. You and your characters have spent a great deal of time together, you know each other intimately, you're old friends – and now you have to say goodbye. Once they're sent out into the cold, uncaring world, your friends might be misjudged, disliked, even criticised. Better to keep them close where you can keep reliving and refining all those lovely moments you've shared ...

Here's the solution: *Get over yourself!*

Give yourself a deadline for changes, tweaks and corrections, meet it, finish up, type THE END and start making new friends – by which I mean start writing another book.

Believe me, I know where you're coming from. I couldn't let go of my first novel, *Telling Stories*. After getting up a 5:00 am every work day for three years and putting in a couple of hours before getting ready for work, I found myself endlessly dithering with it. There were things that needed fixing, certainly, but once they were done I found myself in a sort of never-ending spiral of rewriting for the sake of it. Sometimes I'd make things a tiny bit better, more often I'd make them quite a bit worse and end up using the original version anyway. In the end, I was saved by an advert for a writing contest with a deadline for entries. "Right," I told myself, "I *must* finish by then!" And I did. (Actually, I finished it three days before the deadline, and because I wanted to be shot of the thing, I posted it in to a contest I'd never really intended to enter. It won!)

Here are some other reasons for not letting go.

It has to be perfect

Name one perfect book. Go on, just one. One that no critic has ever expressed the tiniest reservations about, ever. The truth is, there's no such book. Not everyone likes everything, or even the same things. If they did, libraries would consist of hundreds of copies of just a handful of books.

A general anxiety about whether the story works

An author, *especially* a first-time author, can never really judge whether a story works or not, or where its weaknesses are. You need the help of a kindly but disinterested outsider. (See *Get Thee to an Assessor*, below.)

Worry about how people will judge you

Actually, readers don't really think much about the author at all. They're interested in the story and the characters. If they enjoyed the book, they might give your *About the Author* page a cursory glance, but they'll be more interested in looking at your *Also By* page for a dose of more of the same. (Which is why you should start on the next book right away.)

It really is excrement

This happens too sometimes. Hopefully with it's a story, not a whole novel. Again, you're probably not the best judge of this so at least get a second opinion.

But if it has happened and you can't even bring yourself to show it to another living soul, you might like to consider an outrageous concept...

The practise novel

When I first heard someone talk about writing a practise novel, I thought it a bizarre idea. All that time, all that work, *just for practise?* But after that first sharp intake of breath, once I thought about, I wondered why the idea had never occurred to me before.

I have a friend who's a gifted artist. Dave's done a number of my book covers and sold a goodly number of paintings as well. One of the reasons he's so good is that he does it constantly. If he's not working on a major piece, he's sketching and doodling and coming up with ideas. There are videos of some of his sketchbooks online.[1]

One of the barriers to writing freely is thinking about the end game; your audience, what a publisher or critic might think, the way your turn of phrase might be regarded by future generations. But what if there was no end game? What if what you are writing is like the contents of my friend's sketchbook, merely a way of keeping your hand in and working out ideas?

The whole idea of practising writing isn't something that's generally talked about. It's assumed that since everyone is taught to write in school, good writers simply have a natural talent for it. That may or may not be the case, (personally, I think it's more about inclination than talent), but the implication of that idea is that you can never get better. Which is nonsense. We can all run, so how is it that some people can run much faster than the rest of us?

The difference is they're athletes. And what makes an athlete? They practise and train. Constantly.

I've yet to hear of any musician who – never having picked up a guitar or sat down at a keyboard before – did so and mastered it on the spot. Even the infant prodigy Mozart would have had a *plink-ponk-plunk* period. Do you think Michelangelo carved his famous David from a block of stone without spending years chipping away at countless other blocks, refining his technique? The mistakes ended up being turned into gravel paths while David ended up in the Galeria dell'Arccademia in Florence, but only because of Michelangelo's earlier practise.

Perhaps you need to start your novel again and come at it from a different angle, third-person instead of first. Or the whole thing should be seen through the eye of one (or a number) of your characters. Or perhaps you just need to work on something else for a while and come back to this one later. Put it down to practise. There's no shame in that. Learn what you can from it and move on.

> "The only way anybody ever learns to write well is by trying to write well. This usually begins by reading good writing by other people, and writing very badly by yourself, for a long time."
>
> — Ursula K Le Guin

Get thee to an assessor!

This bit will cost money so you'll need to be sure you're ready for it. (Amazing how the prospect of spending hard-earned cash focuses the mind, eh?)

Visit the website of your local writer's association and find their list of manuscript assessors. The better ones are usually affiliated to a professional body of some sort which guarantees a code of conduct and a level of service. Above all, you want a *professional* opinion, not someone who'll take your money and tell you your book is great. (Seriously, there are a lot of sharks out there who'll do just that and try and sign you up to a ridiculously expensive self-publishing contract. Vet them thoroughly first. A Google search is good, or look for them on Writer Beware.[2]

Many writers and editors do manuscript assessments as a sideline so you can check them out beforehand. Obviously, you won't send a young adult novel to someone who specialises in scientific non-fiction, but if you're faced with half a dozen possibilities, visit your local library or bookshop and look through what they've produced. Not everyone likes everyone else's writing so you should find someone with a sympathetic voice.

A manuscript assessor will read your book with a critical eye, point out your strengths and weaknesses, highlight flaws – bits that don't make sense and bits that are really great – consider your characters and plot, and come up with an overall assessment. Is it worth sending off to a publisher yet? Or does it need a bit more work?

Don't be tempted to get a friend or relative to do this for you. For a start, manuscript assessment is a proper job. It's work. At a desk. It's not kicking back with your feet on a stool or browsing the book at bedtime. And you really want the cold hard truth about your writing. A loved one won't have the emotional distance to tell you your masterpiece is crap – or the necessary expertise to say exactly where things went wrong. Publishers and editors may reject your work, but they'll rarely tell you why. (For some of the reasons they may do so, see the next chapter.) You can't work on a weakness unless you know about it. A good assessor will spotlight every bump and glitch.

Let's say the assessment is generally positive. You have a few things to work on, and do so. Now – assuming the assessor is a well-known writer or editor, not some internet unknown whose one-line rating was, "Shit hot!" – you can use that assessment as a lever with a publisher.

When I wrote *Too Many Zeros*, I did just that. I'd never written for the young adult market before so I did some research, read a few YA books, then sent my manuscript off to a well-known YA author and assessor. She found lots of small things and one or two biggies that needed fixing, but her overall assessment was very positive. I made the fixes, popped a couple of lines from her assessment into a cover letter (the good ones, obviously), and sent it off to a publisher along with the first three chapters. A few days later I got a call asking for the rest, and they went on to publish it.

(A quick aside here about assessors. They're not gods and will only suggest changes. It's up to you whether you accept them or not. Most of the time they're spot on, but occasionally I'll make an artistic decision and reject a recommendation. The same goes for editors. It's *your* book, *your* name on the cover. Not theirs.)

Key points from this chapter:

- No writer is a good judge of their own work. Get an independent assessment.
- No writer is a good at spotting their own story's strengths and weaknesses. Get an independent assessment.
- The opinions of relatives and friends can be helpful, but for a thoroughly objective view, get an independent assessment.

Footnotes:
[1] Check Dave's sketchbooks out at **http://www.davidowen.co.nz**. They're under the Videos tab.
[2] Writer Beware: **http://accrispin.blogspot.co.nz**.

12: "Everyone will hate it!"

Critical Overload

*"This is not a book that should be tossed lightly aside.
It should be hurled with great force."*
— Dorothy Parker

So you got a good assessment, made some changes and sent it off to a publisher. Weeks or, most likely, months later you get an email that begins, "Thank you for letting us see this, but I'm afraid that at this time ..."

John Kennedy Toole got a load of those letters. They may have been one of the reasons for his suicide in 1969 at the age of 31. But his mum, after finding a smeared carbon copy of his manuscript, persisted. She got a whole load more, but eventually *A Confederacy of Dunces* was published in 1980. In 1981, it won a Pulitzer Prize, is still in print, and is now hailed as an American classic.

Handling rejection

In the old days, rejection slips would come in the post and writers would plaster their walls with them. They were considered a right of passage, and in many ways they still are – though mostly these days they come by email.

And everybody gets them at one time or another. Everybody.

Despite the fact that J K Rowling had an agent, the first twelve publishers to look at *Harry Potter and the Philosopher's Stone*, (*Sorcerer's Stone* in the US), rejected it. The fact that it was finally accepted by Bloomsbury owes something to the eight-year-old daughter of the company's chairman. After being given the first chapter to read, Alice Newton promptly demanded the rest, catching her father's interest.

Years later, writing under the pseudonym Robert Galbraith, Rowling received another bunch of rejection slips for the first of her detective novels, *The Cuckoo's Calling*.

> "... the first publisher ever to turn down Harry [Potter] wrote Robert [Galbraith] his rudest rejection. So I think it's safe to say I will never write for them. They clearly don't like me, in whatever way I present myself. [Laughs.]"[1]

There are numerous reasons why editors reject work. By far the biggest category is a lack of professionalism. Poor spelling, bad grammar, bad English – such as referring to your work as a "fiction novel" – will all send you straight into the dump bin. Waffly cover letters are another one. Assume you've got 15 seconds to catch an editor's attention. Keep it brief and to the point. You wouldn't tell a prospective employer your wife thinks you're a good worker round the house, so why on earth would you tell a prospective publisher your wife thinks your writing's great? (Unless she happens to be the chair of a Big Five publishing house, of course.) And never, ever send bribes or gifts or inducements. Nothing screams "Amateur!" louder. They're not going to publish your box of chocolates or smiley gift card. They want a story that grips them from the first page; that's going grip book buyers. Remember, publishing is a business, not a charity. Once you send your book off, it's not treated like a rare flower or a delicate glass ornament packed in cotton wool, it's a *product*, one of hundreds or possibly thousands they'll look at this year. At least present it in a professional manner.

> "The book industry is a business. The rejection of your

manuscript is a business decision. It is not personal."[2]

But even when you've done all the work, and got an assessment, and turned in the very best piece of writing you can, there are many other reasons you may be rejected. Did you send it to the right place? A romance publisher's unlikely to go for hard-boiled science fiction. A children's publisher may not appreciate your erotica. (This kind of thing happens more often than you'd credit!)

The publisher may be looking for something specific. A love story, perhaps, or a tear-jerker. They follow trends too. If boy wizards, or zombies, or teenage vampires are suddenly a Big Thing, many will try to catch onto the coattails of the current craze. (This does *not* mean you should ever "write to market". Ever. Not least because by the time you're finished the market will almost certainly have moved on.)

The publisher may have budgetary constraints or reached their limit for new books for this quarter or this year. They may have recently accepted a novel similar to your own or reached some other quota. In recalling her early struggles to get published, prolific romance novelist Nora Roberts said:

> "I received my manuscript back with a nice little note which said that my work showed promise, and the story had been very entertaining and well done. But that they already had their American writer."[3]

Not everyone likes every story. Ever picked up a promising looking book, read the first paragraph and put it down again? Editors are no different. Editorial choice is a personal thing. What works for one may not work for another.

When he was in my home town for the local launch of his book *Atlantic*, non-fiction author Simon Winchester recounted how his breakthrough book, *The Surgeon of Crowthorne* (known in North America as *The Professor and the Madman*), made it into print.

His proposal was lying in the bin of the editor who'd reviewed it. Another editor visited, plucked it out and looked it through while the first finished his phone call.

"What's this?" the second asked when the first finished his call.

"Oh, someone wants to write a book on lexicography. You can't sell lexicography."

"I bet I could."

"I bet you couldn't."

"Right, you're on!"

Second ed won the bet. The book sold more than three million copies.

If this sounds a brutal and rather random process, it is, but it's the way the business works. Get used to it. Just don't take it personally. They're rejecting a bunch of words on a page, not *you*.

Or think of it like this: rejection isn't feedback, it's market research ...

> "This manuscript of yours that has just come back from another editor is a precious package. Don't consider it rejected. Consider that you've addressed it 'to the editor who can appreciate my work' and it has simply come back stamped 'Not at this address'. Just keep looking for the right address."
> — *Barbara Kingsolver*

You're not alone!

Here are a few famous rejection notes, who received them, and the book they were aimed at ...

"Stick to teaching."

Louisa May Alcott,
Little Women

"An irresponsible holiday story that will never sell."

Kenneth Grahame,
The Wind In The Willows

"I haven't the foggiest idea about what the man is trying to say. Apparently the author intends it to be funny."

Joseph Heller,
Catch-22

"An absurd and uninteresting fantasy which was rubbish and dull."

William Golding,
The Lord Of The Flies

"An absurd story as romance, melodrama or record of New York high life."

F Scott Fitzgerald,
The Great Gatsby

"We feel that we don't know the central character well enough."

J D Salinger,
The Catcher In The Rye

"Hopelessly bogged down and unreadable."

Ursula K Le Guin,
The Left Hand of Darkness

"I rack my brains why a chap should need thirty pages to describe how he turns over in bed before going to sleep."

Marcel Proust,
In Search of Lost Time
(AKA Remembrance of Things Past)

*"We are not interested in science fiction

*which deals with negative utopias.
They do not sell."*

Stephen King,
Carrie

(If you'd like to see some more famous/infamous rejection slips, check out these links: **http://bit.ly/2xrLGqk** and **http://bit.ly/2mscIfu**.)

Another sort of lottery

If publishing seems like something of a lottery (and it is), there's another, more pernicious, sort of lottery you can indulge in and, most likely, get rejected by: writing contests.

They're valuable, don't get me wrong. They certainly have a place in encouraging writers and revealing new talent. Winning one is great publicity and might even get you a toe-hold with a publisher, just don't take them too seriously. Why? *Because there can only be one winner.*

In theory at least, a publisher receiving five fantastic manuscripts can publish them all – in effect, declare five winners – but in a contest, four would have to lose. There's only one Man Booker prize each year, only one Edgar Allan Poe Award, and only one Engineer Mohammed Bashir Karaye Prize for Hausa Writing (seriously!).

Contests are typically advertised as being judged by Big Name Writer, but often BNW won't sift through a thousand (or ten thousand) manuscripts. A selection panel will filter out the obvious dross, then whittle down the remainder to something manageable. Perhaps ten or twenty entries for the shortlist. BNW will then select from that selection. It's entirely possible that, given *all* the entries, BNW would have selected something else entirely.

Even the big contests have a lottery aspect. Sam Leith, one of the 2015 Man Booker judges, wrote:

"As one of my fellow judges commented in the Man Booker

shortlist meeting, this was the point at which the gameshow aspects of a book prize start to take over: we took a list of 13 first-rate novels and halved it for no other reason than that's the way the game works. Tonight, we single out but one."[4]

So keep a sense of perspective. If you win, fantastic, but if you don't, don't take it as any sort of critique of your writing.

Key points from this chapter:

- Not everyone loves every book or story.
- Every writer worth their salt has had rejections. Take heart from some of the more famous ones.
- Enter contests with caution. There can only be one winner. Not winning doesn't mean your writing's rubbish.

Footnotes:

[1] J K Rowling interview:
http://www.theguardian.com/books/2015/nov/28/conversation-lauren-laverne-jk-rowling-interview.
[2] LitRejections website: **http://www.litrejections.com**.
[3] Nora Roberts' early writing career:
http://en.wikipedia.org/wiki/Nora_Roberts#Beginning.
[4] Judging the Man Booker Prize, 2015:
http://www.theguardian.com/books/2015/oct/13/man-booker-prize-2015-one-judge-on-the-impossible-task-of-choosing-a-winner.

Bonus Chapter

"You can't say, I won't write today because that excuse will extend into several days, then several months, then you are not a writer any more, just someone who dreams about being a writer."
— Dorothy C Fontana

This chapter is a collection of thoughts about writing, the writing process and an insight into the way I work. Like the rest of this book, it's just my humble opinion. Take from it what you will.

Write what you love

You're going to spend countless hours together, so why would you work on something you don't really care about, something that doesn't interest or inspire you? If you're really not that bothered about your characters, why would Jo Random-Reader care about them?

Engage and entertain yourself first, and you might just do the same for readers.

One of the common (misguided) recommendations to new writers is what I call *genre chasing*. A romance between a teenage vampire and a human makes it big on the charts, and suddenly everyone's writing them. But one of the reasons that *Twilight* took the world by storm back in 2003 was *because* no one had done that sort of story before.

Its author, Stephanie Meyer, wrote it for her own enjoyment, and only sent off to a few agents after being persuaded to do so by her sister. (In a throwback to Chapter 12, five didn't bother to respond, nine rejected it, but one took it on. Meyer eventually landed a US$750,000 contract for three books.)

The root word of originality is *original*.

Certainly, other publishers try to cash in when a new trend emerges, typically by dredging up stuff from their backlist. If you try to dive in and write one from scratch, even once its accepted, you're looking at a lead time of around a year before the book hits the shelves, by which time the craze may well be over.

Yes, publishers keep one eye on what's selling now, but – like Mad-Eye Moody from the Harry Potter books – the other's casting about looking for the Next Big Thing.

(Another footnote about *Twilight*. I once talked to an editor from a large San Francisco publishing house that specialised in books for children and young adults. She told me that when *Twilight* hit the bestseller charts, she and her fellow editors all read it and all agreed that if they'd picked the manuscript from the slush pile, it would have gone straight into the bin.

> *"Write a book you'd like to read. If you wouldn't read it, why would anybody else? Don't write for a perceived audience or market. It may well have vanished by the time your book's ready."*
>
> — Hilary Mantel

Treat it like a business

If you're an artist with a capital A, or can only work when possessed by the Muse, you might like to skip this bit and go back to Chapter 6.

Parkinson's Law reckons that "Work expands so as to fill the time available for its completion," and that's particularly true of writing. Right now I'm aware of a certain lassitude as I reach the end of this volume, having originally budgeted a week for its completion and almost reaching the end after just three days. What's more, it's a lovely sunny morning and I've got plenty of time in hand ...

No, no, no!

It's not as if I haven't been here before. I spent 18 years writing a monthly column for a computer magazine, and virtually every one of them was composed in a flat panic in the day or two before deadline. I'd despatch the columns with a sigh of relief on the morning they were due and tell myself that next month it would all be different. I'd plan properly, start early and cruise towards the deadline. Yet somehow I never did.

There's another old business saying that applies equally well to writing: "If you want something in a hurry or done well, give it to a busy man."

Writing requires a certain amount of discipline – the same sort of discipline that drags you into work each day – and I find it useful to incorporate some of that discipline into my writing routine. For a start, I keep a timesheet. I record start time and end times each day, with one minus the other equalling the hours and minutes worked. It's simple to set up on a spreadsheet, and at the end of the week I can total up to see how much I've done.

Apart from the psychological trick of telling myself that I'm "on the clock" now so no dilly-dallying around, it also gives me useful information about how long things actually take. And that means I can make plans in advance.

The second part of my "not-really-work work system" involves weekly meetings; fifteen or twenty minutes on a Monday morning in which I review what I achieved the week before and plan for where I want to go in the week ahead. (My notes for this week include finishing the first draft of this book, an allowance for writing-related reading – as opposed to reading for pleasure – and time for blogging and general admin.) I also use it to set a target word count for the week, and this too helps keep me on track.

Knowing how quickly you can produce work – even rough first drafts – is useful in itself, but it also means you can challenge yourself. At present, my peak writing speed is 500-600 words per hour, with an average of around 400. I'd really like to get to double that, which may sound a lot but it's still only one word every 4.5 seconds. (In comparison, most of us speak at about 150 words a minute; the equivalent of 9,000 words an hour.) So by measuring and testing and pushing myself a little each day, I'm slowly (very slowly!) getting quicker. Whether I ever reach my goal or not remains to be seen, but what's the worst that can happen? Maybe I'll fail miserably and only ever average 600 words an hour. That's still 50% better than my current rate and a "failure" I could live with.

A very important footnote

Despite the workman-like routine outlined above, I *never* regard writing as proper work. It's fun! Always!

I regard writing the next book in the same way that climbers regard mountains: they're a challenge. You tackle them simply because they're there.

Yes, the going can be difficult at times, and frustrating, and sometimes a bit of a slog – which is where a little self-discipline can help. Sometimes you'll take a wrong turning, hit an impassable barrier and have to backtrack. Sometimes conditions will conspire against you and you'll have try again another day. But when you finally make it, there's nothing quite like reaching that pinnacle you've set sights on all this time. And when you do, you'll find yourself shielding your eyes and casting about, looking around for the next challenge.

Become a guinea pig

That brings me on to something every writer should do, always, and especially when they're still finding their feet: experiment; test yourself; try new things. According to the late Arthur C Clarke: "The only way of discovering the limits of the possible is to venture a little way past them into the impossible."[1] I'm trying to do that with my writing speed, but there are countless other things you can experiment with.

What time do you work best? Morning, midday, late at night? How do you know? Have you tried an early start, or a late one? How many times have you heard people say, "I never thought I could do that," after they'd discovered they could?

Japanese author Haruki Murakami has a punishing writing routine:

> "When I'm in writing mode for a novel, I get up at four a.m. and work for five to six hours. In the afternoon, I run for ten kilometres or swim for fifteen hundred meters (or do both), then I read a bit and listen to some music. I go to bed at nine p.m. I keep to this routine every day without variation. The repetition itself becomes the important thing; it's a form of mesmerism. I mesmerize myself to reach a deeper state of mind. But to hold to such repetition for so long—six months to a year—requires a good amount of mental and physical strength. In that sense, writing a long novel is like survival training. Physical strength is as necessary as artistic sensitivity."[2]

Some authors, such as Stephen King, love loud music while they work and can't wait to slip on the headphones each day. (Personally, I find anything with lyrics distracting.) Some find office noise and bustle helpful. (In which case, try Coffitivity – www.coffitivity.com. It recreates the background buzz of a cafe.)

I'd never considered myself a morning person till I worked out that 5:00—7:00 am was really the only consistent time I'd get to work each workday. To compensate, I took up meditation to help me through the day. A 20-minute session roughly compensated for the missing hours and I'd catch up fully at the weekend. Now, even though my time is freer, I'm still at my desk by 6:00 am.

There is no "right way" to write. Everyone's different. But the only way you'll find what works best for you is to use yourself as a guinea pig.

Do a Nanowrimo

On the subject of experiments, Nanowrimo is something every writer should try at least once in their lives. You might "fail" miserably and only write 25,000 words in a month. (How many did you do last month?) But you just might learn a whole new way of working.

I did.

Technically, Nanowrimo should be written NaNoWriMo as it originally stood for National Novel Writing Month. These days it's international and hundreds of thousands of people take part.

Nanowrimo runs from 1 November to 30 November each year, and the aim is simple: you must write 50,000 words of a novel in those 30 days – an average pace of 1,667 words every day. Entry is free, it's all self-managed, and there's no one hanging over your shoulder checking what you write makes sense. If you say you've written 50,000 words on Day 1, you'll be declared a winner. If you write "the the the" 50,000 times, you'll be declared a winner. (Everyone who makes it to 50,000 words is a winner. If you want to cheat, the only person you're really cheating is yourself.)

You shouldn't start writing before 1 November, but you are allowed to prepare. You can do extensive plotting, work on your characters and character arcs, make notes about subplots, maguffins, backgrounds, worlds and all the rest. Or you could do what I did a few years ago; start with a blank screen.

I'd always thought of myself as a plotter, not a pantser (see Chapter 3), and had long envied people like Ian Rankin and Lee Child who just sit down and start writing. So I decided to give it bash. With no preparation other than the thought I might try to write a romance, (because they're supposed to be "easy", hah), I sat down on the morning of 1 November 2013 and wrote the first thing that came into my head. It was the word "Bastards!"

What emerged amazed me. Not a living, breathing, sassy character in the form of Jane Child, but a whole plot too. And sub-plots. I hasten to add these didn't appear in a blinding flash of illumination, but the whole thing did have a sense of direction. Finding out exactly what that was brought me back to my desk every day. It was exactly like this:

> "It's like driving a car at night. You never see further than your headlights, but you can make the whole trip that way."
> — E L Doctrow

The story that emerged was more thriller than romance, (romantic-suspense, perhaps), and kept me entranced. So much so that by the end of the month, when I'd reached 50,000 words and was declared a winner along with tens of thousands of other participants, I carried on at the same pace for another three weeks, ending up with an 80,000-word novel.

Still a little stunned at what I'd done and not really believing it could ever be anything but a freewriting exercise or a practise novel, (see Chapter 11), I printed it out, tossed it in a drawer, and got on with something else. Two months later, I took a tentative look at it and discovered to my amazement that it was pretty good. Actually, really good. Oh, it needed some work. Bits needed shifting around. Some things needed trimming, some expanding, but the story as a whole was a ripper. The climax even had *me* turning the pages – and I'd written it!

I did a second draft, put it out to some trusted beta readers who made some invaluable suggestions which I incorporated into a third draft, and that book is now available in print and ebook. (It's called *Private Viewing*[3]. As I write this, a second book in the series is about to hit the shelves. It's called *Private Lives*[4].)

The point is not to advertise it – although I'm sure you'll really enjoy it(!) – but to say that it would never have been written if I hadn't tried "pantsing" – something I firmly believed I could never do. The experience, after more than twenty years of writing, was a revelation. I've since written another novel like that, (*Payback*, during Nanowrimo 2014), and part of my planning for the week after I finish the first draft of this book is to start on the fourth part of my *Forty Million Minutes* series. I've no idea where it will lead, but I can't wait to find out!

Footnote

You don't have to wait for November to have a Nanowrimo month. You might miss out on the support, the encouraging graphing software and the prospect of being an official "winner", but you can declare one at any time. Set a target of 50,000 words for whatever month you choose and keep a daily word count. If your target month happens to have 31 days, you'll have it easy – a mere 1,613 words each day. But beware of February because you'll be looking at 1,786 words a day – unless it's a leap year, in which case you'll only have to average 1,724 words. You could even call it *Nanowrimo practise!*

Wearing two hats

One of the advantages of a career in the IT industry and a background of writing and commentating on it is that it gives you an appreciation of how quickly things change. And not just in IT but in the world.

When I first started as a help columnist in the mid-1990s, readers wrote us letters. Actual physical letters delivered by a postman. And we sent letters in reply. I used to have a stack of *PC World* letterhead and reply-paid envelopes. I'd print off answers to readers' problems on my dot-matrix printer and pop them in the mailbox up the road. My monthly columns went by mail too, on 3.5-inch floppy disks to my editor.

Writing hasn't changed, nor have the problems writers face in getting their stories down and knocking them into a passable shape, but the industry around them has changed dramatically and continues to do so. I recently heard an established writer railing against these changes. For years he'd made a good income from his work, then X went bust, Y was discontinued, and Z merged with MegaCorp and didn't want him any more. He was bitter and disappointed. "It's not like the old days ..."

He's right, it's not. It's not even like November 18, 2007, the day before Amazon's first Kindle was released and kick-started the ebook revolution.[5] (Ten years on, the publishing industry as a whole is still reeling from that.) But listening to him, I wondered if he'd even heard of indie publishing. He's a reasonably well-known figure, has a large body of work behind him to which, presumably, he still retains the rights, so why not? What's he got to lose?

If you want to make an income from writing, now more than ever, it's a case of adapt and change, or die.

As a writer, I wear two hats. By far the biggest is the hard-hat, the one I put on for mining words and slaving at the coal face, but there's a smaller one too, a neat little Fedora that I usually only don for an hour or two each week. It's my business hat. Wearing it, I follow blogs and news and keep myself apprised of what's happening in the world of publishing. It's an interest, but it's also an important part of what I hope one day to make a proper writing business. If I'm ever going to make a living from this lark, I need to keep abreast of what's going on!

Whether or not you feel a need to keep up to date as I do, one thing you should always be open to is learning. There's always more to discover about writing, always room to improve your technique or polish your style. There are courses, of course, but there's also that ancient, time-honoured method called reading. I read widely, fiction and non-fiction, across a broad range of genres. I love words and I'm curious about what people like, what works, what doesn't, and why. Some popular writers leave me cold, others I devour. There's no such thing as a truly bad book, only one that doesn't work for me. Those that don't ring my bell can be great to learn from: *Why have I suddenly lost interest? What's wrong with this character? Why does that description jar?*

Another way of keeping up to date is to join a writers' group. There are many national bodies, some general, some specialist (such as romance- or thriller-specific groups), and many internet gatherings besides. Whether you prefer face-to-face or Facebook, the contact with like-minded souls and the interchange of ideas, likes and dislikes can be illuminating.

"Writing is lonely work. Try meeting regularly with a small

group of other writers to remind yourself why you hate everyone."

— *James Thurber*

The three Ps

If you've made it this far through this book, the three Ps above pretty much sum up my advice.

Practise

Whether writing's an innate skill or one that can be acquired is a debate for another place. What is certain is that any skill can be improved with practise, whether it's rock climbing, roller skating or writing. So practise!

> *"You don't start out writing good stuff. You start out writing crap and thinking it's good stuff, and then gradually you get better at it. That's why I say one of the most valuable traits is persistence."*
>
> — *Octavia Butler*

Productivity

Practise means producing stuff, and as I hope you've discovered through all these reasons for *not* writing, (or not continuing, or not finishing), that we're often our own worst enemies. The solution is simple: chip out a small portion of your day – even a half-hour will do – and write a few paragraphs. Produce something, resist the Resistance, and remember the maths:

```
300 words per day x 5 days per week
    = 1 novel this time next year
```

Professionalism

No one cares what your first draft looks like, or your second, or you third, but they do begin to care when you present your work to the world. Always, always, always do so in a professional manner. It's still the main reason stories and books get rejected: can't spell, can't punctuate, bad grammar, cliched writing ... And if, despite dotting all the Is and crossing all the Ts, your submissions still come back unwanted, remember the fourth P: Persistence. Think of J K Rowling and the publishers who turned her down (both as Rowling and as Robert Galbraith). Think of the fourteen rejects Stephanie Meyer got and the fifteenth agent who made her a household name. Think of John Kennedy Toole, giving up in despair, only to win a posthumous Pulitzer Prize. Persistence beats Resistance.

Being a successful writer

Success is a odd concept when you think about it. What does it *really* mean? Does it mean selling truckloads of books, or merely making a living as a writer? Does it mean acclaim from critics and academics? Having a New York Times bestseller? Winning prizes – a Pulitzer, a Hugo, a Gold Dagger, or the Man Booker? Or does it mean simply finding a publisher for your manuscript?

The truth is that success means different things to different people at different times in their careers, but the key thing about it is that it's a concept that comes from within, *not* from without.

An example: I know of one famous writer who's had bestsellers for years, makes a very good living from his work, gets rave reviews and has a huge fan-base, but I get the feeling that what he really craves is academic acclaim, mention in learned journals, perhaps even some sort of prize for Literature (with a capital L). To the world outside, he's a huge success; to himself, not so much.

What are your own criteria for success? They'll change as you grow and develop as a writer, but it's worth picking them out and celebrating them, even in a small way, even if it's just giving yourself a pat on the back.

For my own part, simply typing THE END on the last page of my very first novel was a mark of success. I'd done it! *I'd actually written a book!* Once that delight subsided, my next measure of success became getting the book into a shape and form that I was happy for other people to look at. Then it became finding a publisher. (Actually, it won a prize first.) Then it was getting it published. Then having a book launch, then getting reviews ...[6]

In some ways, this ties back to the using-systems-not-goals idea we explored way back in Chapter 1 (under *The Fallacy of Goal Setting*). If you keep your definition of success modest and achievable, then gradually expand it, you're more likely to stay on track. There's quite a difference between 'I'll be successful if I sell a million books' and 'I'll be successful if I finish the first draft.' Remember, even the likes of Lee Child and Stephen King once went, 'Wow, I can't believe it. I've actually finished writing a whole novel!'

So think about what *you* would like to achieve as a writer – whether it's just finishing an autobiography for other members of your family, writing enough short stories to fill a book, or completing the first part of a multi-volume, galaxy-spanning saga – break the task down into a series of "success steps", then celebrate each one along the way.

You ask me why I spend my life writing?
Do I find entertainment?
Is it worthwhile?
Above all, does it pay?
If not, then, is there a reason? ...
I write only because
There is a voice within me
That will not be still.

— Sylvia Plath, 1948 (age 16)

Footnotes:

[1] In fact, it's one of Clarke's Three Laws (see **http://en.wikipedia.org/wiki/Clarke%27s_three_laws**). He also proposed what he called Clarke's 69th Law which reads, "Reading computer manuals without the hardware is as frustrating as reading sex manuals without the software. In both cases the cure is simple though usually very expensive."

[2] **http://www.theparisreview.org/interviews/2/the-art-of-fiction-no-182-haruki-murakam**.

[3] *Private Viewing*, by Geoff Palmer is available here: **http://geoffpalmer.co.nz/htwab11**.

[4] *Private Lives*, by Geoff Palmer is available here: **http://geoffpalmer.co.nz/htwab12**.

[5] The first Kindles sold for US$399. Amazon wildly underestimated demand for them. The first batch sold out in a little over five hours and they were out of stock till April 2008.

[6] The book was *Telling Stories* (**http://geoffpalmer.co.nz/htwab13**). It won the Reed Fiction Award for the Best Unpublished Novel in 1995 and was first published in 1996.

Appendix 1

A handy word-count table

Here's something you might find useful; a words-per-hour table broken down into words-per-minute, along with the average number of seconds taken between each word. For example, if you wrote 300 words in the last hour, you averaged five words per minute, or one word every 12 seconds. If you catch yourself thinking, "What, only one word every 12 seconds? I can do better than that!" then you've discovered one of the uses for this table.

(By way of comparison, average conversation speed is 150 – 200 words *per minute*, which equates to 9,000 – 12,000 words per hour.)

Words per hour	Words per minute	Seconds between each word
100	1.7	36.0
200	3.3	18.0
300	5.0	12.0
400	6.7	9.0
500	8.3	7.2
600	10.0	6.0
700	11.7	5.1
800	13.3	4.5
900	15.0	4.0
1,000	16.7	3.6
1,100	18.3	3.3
1,200	20.0	3.0
1,300	21.7	2.8
1,400	23.3	2.6
1,500	25.0	2.4
1,600	26.7	2.3
1,700	28.3	2.1
1,800	30.0	2.0
1,900	31.7	1.9
2,000	33.3	1.8

About the Author

Geoff Palmer is a writer, which is astonishingly convenient as you appear to be a reader! He's climbed mountains in Africa, picked grapes in Switzerland, sold cameras in London, programmed computers in Fiji, and spent eight years working as a professional photographer. He's also quite tall.

Geoff's first novel, *Telling Stories*, won the Reed Fiction Award, and in 20+ years of freelance technical writing he's won four Qantas Media Awards and been a finalist for Columnist of the Year. His second novel, *Too Many Zeros*, was published by Penguin in 2011, and a number of other novels have followed since.

He writes, every day if he can, subject to the demands of his cat, who regards him as her personal servant, portable cushion and entertainment centre. In return, she allows him to share her house in Wellington, New Zealand.

You'll find him on:
facebook.com/geoffpalmerNZ
twitter.com/geoffpalmer

Or at:
www.geoffpalmer.co.nz

If you enjoyed this book, please consider leaving an online review. They really help writers!

Also by Geoff Palmer

Telling Stories
Payback

BLUEBELLE INVESTIGATIONS:
Private Viewing
Private Lives

FORTY MILLION MINUTES:
Too Many Zeros
Lair of the Sentinels
The Man with the Missing Jaw
The Shadow Behind the Stars

About the Reader

Yes, you!

Actually, I don't know much about you except that we seem to share this weird passion for writing. Was this book any use to you? Were there bits you hated, bits you liked, things I missed, or things you didn't understand? I'd love to know. Feel free to drop me a line at the email address below.

Perhaps you'd like to try some of my other books or keep an eye on what I'm up to via my (very) occasional newsletter. You'll find details of both on my website: **http://geoffpalmer.co.nz**.

Oh, and one more thing: thanks for reading this book!

Geoff
geoff@geoffpalmer.co.nz

INDEX

"??", using as a placeholder 28, 44

A

ability 25, 31, 71, 91
accuracy 42, 43
A Christmas Carol 16, 37, 38, 80
Adele 83
Alcott, Louisa May 104
Alice in Wonderland 37
Allende, Isabelle 57
Amazon 10, 116, 121
Anderson, Kevin J 44
Anti-Social (program) 27
As I Lay Dying 80, 82
assessors, manuscript 96, 98-100
Astounding Science Fiction 71

B

Bach, Richard 48
background 42-47, 68
basic plots 36
basic tools 1
Beatles, The 49
Beckett, Samuel 95
Bell Jar, The 65
Bergler, Edumnd 83
Bingham, Harry 93

blockers (software) 26
Bloomsbury 102
Booker, Christopher 36, 37, 41
Bradbury, Malcolm 41
Bridget Jones's Diary 37
Brontë, Charlotte 36-38
Burgess, 65
Business Insider 12
business of writing, the 52, 55, 81, 110, 117
Butler, Octavia 118

C

calendar, for writing 18, 61, 63
carbon paper 23
Carré, John le 36
Carrie 106
Carroll, Lewis 37
Catch-22 105
Catcher In The Rye, The 105
Chandler, Raymond 79
characters 42, 43, 44, 45, 47, 54, 55, 64, 67, 71, 91, 95, 96, 98, 99, 105, 109, 114, 117
character checklist 38-39, 41
character consistency 39
character development 43-44, 55, 67

129

character foreshadowing 89
character names 29
character sheets 38-39
characters and situations 38
checklist, writing classes 54
Chekov, Anton 88
Chekov's Gun 88, 89, 91
Chicago Manual of Style, The 29
Child, Jane 114
Child, Lee 1-3, 34, 42-44, 46, 47, 54, 81, 114, 120
Clarke, Arthur C 112, 121
classes, writing 37, 50, 51, 53
Coffitivity (website) 113
Cold Turkey (program) 26
Confederacy of Dunces, A 101
contest, writing 96, 106, 107
correct ways of writing 39
"creative difficulties" 83-84
creative mode 90
Crillo, Francesco 19
Cuckoo's Calling, The 102

D

Dickens, Charles 22, 24, 37, 38, 45, 46, 67, 80
discipline 50, 62, 111
distractions, general 19, 31, 60, 83
distractions, solutions 26-31
distractions, sneaky 28, 66
Doctrow, E L 115

Doorway Effect, the 24, 25
Dostoevsky, Fyodor 24
draft, zero 68, 69, 78
draft, first 7, 20, 34, 43, 67-73, 78, 92, 95, 111, 119, 120

E

Earthly Powers 65
Edgar Allan Poe Award 106
editing mode 90
Engineer Mohammed Bashir Karaye Prize for Hausa Writing 106
essential tools 1-2
Eugenides, Jeffrey 64
Eyre, Jane 36, 38

F

Facebook 10, 13, 22, 26, 27, 30, 117, 125
fantasy (fiction) 47, 52, 55, 79
Faulkner, William 64, 80
Fielding, Helen 37
finishing, not 95, 118
first drafts 7, 43, 67, 68, 71, 72, 73, 92, 95, 111, 115, 119, 120
Fitzgerald, F Scott 83, 105
Fontana, Dorothy C 109
foreshadowing 89, 91
Fowles, John 40, 41, 65
Freedom (program) 26

Freewrite (smart typewriter) 28
freewriting 68, 85, 87, 115
French Lieutenant's Woman, The 40
futzing 30

G

Galbraith, Robert 102, 119
Galeria dell'Arccademia 98
genre 44, 47, 80, 84, 109, 117
genre chasing 109
Getting Started 5, 67
goal setting 14, 16, 60, 112, 120
Gold Dagger Award 119
Golding, William 105
Goodreads 42, 44, 47
Google Maps 42
Grahame, Kenneth 104
grammar 48, 49, 52, 102, 119
grammar checking 30, 31
Grant, Jim (see: Child, Lee)
Great Gatsby, The 105
Great Tradition, The 49
GUI interface 23

H

hardware, computer 26-28, 121
Harry Potter 38, 102, 110
Harry Potter and the Philosopher's Stone 102
hats, wearing two 116, 117
Heinlein, Robert 5, 73

Heinlein's Rules for Writers 70, 72
Heller, Joseph 42, 105
Hemingway, Ernest 72, 86
Hendrix, Jimi 49
His Dark Materials 84
historical fiction 44
Hugo Award 119
Hulu 10, 27

I

insanity, avoiding 2, 3
In Search of Lost Time 105
indie publishing 117
intention statements 17, 18, 21

J

journaling 85, 87
judgement of others 40, 96, 100
Juvenal 1

K

Kafka, Franz 2
keeping going 75
keeping up to date 117
Killing Floor 1
Kindle 116
King, Stephen 106, 113, 120
Kingsolver, Barbara 104
Kite, Tom 22

L

Lamott, Anne 61, 92
Leavis, F R 49
Left Hand of Darkness, The 105
Le Guin, Ursula K L 98, 105
Leith, Sam 106
Lennon, John 50, 56
Letting Go 93
LibreOffice (word-processor) 27
literary fiction 52
literature 61, 79, 119
LitRejections (website) 107
Little Women 104
London, Jack 33
Long Goodbye, The 82
Lord of the Flies, The 105
Lord of the Rings, The 31, 37
lost time, tracking down 9
Loterzo, Kat 20

M

Macbeth 37
Magus, The 65
Man Booker Prize 106, 107, 119
Mantel, Hilary 46, 47, 66, 85, 110
manuscript assessors 96, 98-100
Marquez, Gabriel Garcia 65
Martian, The 65
Martin, Andy 3, 34, 41

Martin Chuzzlewit 80
Maugham, W Somerset 59
Mayle, Peter 75
McCartney, Paul 49, 56
Melville, Herman 83
Meyer. Stephanie 109, 119
Michelangelo 98
Middlesex 64
Moby Dick 83
Mozart, Amadeus 98
multitasking 25, 31
Muses, the 61, 62
myths;
    - goal setting 14
    - multitasking 25
    - not practicing 81
    - slow writing 99

N

Nanowrimo 114-116
"necessary distance" 69, 70
Neutronium Alchemist, The 45
Newton, Alice 102
Night's Dawn Trilogy 44, 82
non-fiction 2, 43, 99, 103, 117
Novel Today, The 41

O

one-draft writers 42, 70, 72
One Hundred Years of Solitude 65
Online Etymology (website) 32

opening lines 46, 64, 66
Our Mutual Friend 46
overview 2

P

Palmer, Geoff 32, 43, 121, 127
pantsers 34, 41, 114
Parker, Dorothy 89, 101
Parkinson's Law 110
PC World 117
perfection, the quest for 69, 73, 92, 95, 96
Plath, Sylvia 65, 120
placeholders ("??") 28, 44
plotters 34, 41, 114
Pomodoro Technique 18-20, 21, 31, 82
practise, writing 72, 80, 81, 98, 116, 118
practise novel, the 97, 115
Pratchett, Terry 83
Presley, Elvis 49
Pressfield, Stephen 58, 63, 78
Private Lives 115, 121
Private Viewing 115, 121
production targets 60, 62
productivity 118
professionalism 102, 118, 119
Professor and the Madman, The 103
Proust, Marcel 105
Pulitzer Prize 101, 119
Pullman, Philip 84

Q

qualifications 48

R

Rankin, Ian 34, 114
Reacher, Jack 34
Reed Fiction Award 121, 125
rejection, handling 101, 102, 104
rejection, reasons for 102, 103, 119
rejection slips 101, 102
rejections, famous 106
Remembrance of Things Past 105
research 29, 42-44, 46, 47
Resistance 58, 59, 62, 78, 87, 118, 119
rewriting 52, 70-72, 89, 90, 96
Robb, J D (see also Roberts, Nora) 81
Roberts, Nora 81, 103, 107
romance fiction and writers 37, 50, 52, 79, 80, 103, 114, 115
Rowling, J K 54, 101, 102, 107, 119

S

Safire, William 52
Salinger, J D 105
Sarton, May 7
Schulz, Charles M 83

science fiction (sci-fi) 47, 50, 70, 71, 79, 81, 103, 105
Science of Science Fiction Writing, The 71
Scrooge, Ebenezer 38
Second Bakery Attack, The 64
secrets of writing 7, 34, 48, 54, 58, 66, 67, 68, 88, 91
Seinfeld, Jerry 60, 87
self-awareness 59
self-defeating practices 14, 60
self-discipline 112
self-doubt 77
self-publishing 99
setting 46
seven basic plots, the 36, 40, 41
Seven Basic Plots: Why We Tell Stories, The 36, 41
Shakespeare, William 37
slow writing, myth 79-81, 89
Smith, Dean Wesley 81
software, computer 7, 26, 116, 121
spell-checking 30, 31
spelling 39, 68, 102
St. Crow, Lili 62
stepping back 69, 70
Stephenson, Neal 79, 82
Street View (Google) 42
successful writer, being a 119, 120
Surgeon of Crowthorne, The 103
systems (not goals) 16-17, 120

T

Telling Stories 66, 96, 121
The Most Dangerous Writing App (website) 86
Thurber, James 77, 118
ticking clock, the 7
time, carving out some 20
time, tracking down lost 9
timeanddate.com (website) 61
timesheet, keeping 9, 21, 90, 111
tomato, writing with a 18-20
Toole, John Kennedy 101, 119
Too Many Zeros 35, 36, 40, 41, 100, 125
Twain, Mark 88
Twilight 109, 110
Twitter 10, 27, 30
typewriter 2, 23, 28, 31

U

Ubuntu (operating system) 27
uncertainty 3, 77

V

Vimeo 27

W

wall, hitting the 77, 88
War and Peace 22
War of Art, The 58, 63, 78

War of the Worlds, The 36, 78
weaving stories 39
weekly meetings 111
Weir, Andy 65, 67
White, E B 59
Winchester, Simon 103
Wolf Hall 46
word-count table 122-123
word processor 24, 26-28, 30
workshops 50, 53-56

world-building 44, 45, 46, 47
writer's block 83, 84, 87
writing, secrets 7, 34, 48, 54, 58, 66, 67, 68, 88, 91
Writer Beware (website) 99, 100
WYSIWYG 23, 68

Y

YouTube 14, 27

Printed in Great Britain
by Amazon